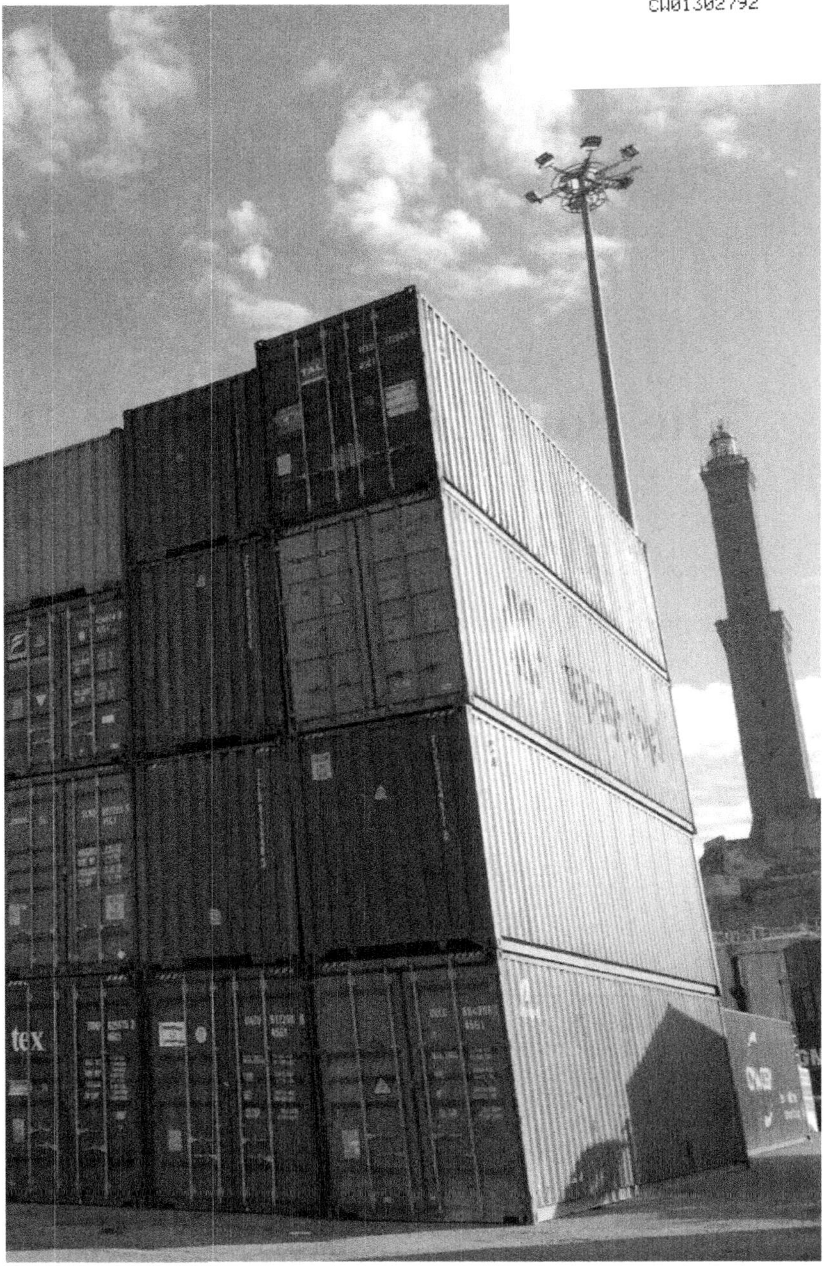
tex

The Port-Crime Interface

A Report on Organised Crime & Corruption in

Seaports

Dr Anna Sergi[1]

University of Essex,

---

[1] The author can be contacted at asergi@essex.ac.uk. The author is thankful to Co-Investigator, Dr Luca Storti, for his comments on earlier drafts of this report and to Ms Sara Noto, intern at the Centre for Criminology at the University of Essex in Autumn 2019 for her support with some initial data gathering.

To all the people met on these journeys, to all the colourful containers, to the open waters.

London 2020

Photo: Melbourne March 2019, Author's rights

Table of content

THE RESEARCH PROJECT	**10**
EXECUTIVE SUMMARY – AT A GLANCE	**15**
ORGANISED CRIME AND THE WATERFRONT: AN INTRODUCTION	**24**
OVERVIEW: PORT ECONOMY AND MARITIME SECURITY	**32**
ORGANISED CRIME IN PORTS: TRAFFICKING, CORRUPTION AND GOVERNANCE	**39**
CASE STUDY 1 GENOVA, ITALY	**48**
GENERAL INFORMATION	49
POLICE AND SECURITY AUTHORITIES	50
ILLICIT TRAFFICKING	51
DRUG TRAFFICKING	51
OTHER ILLICIT TRADE	55
WHAT FURTHER THINGS CAN WE LEARN FROM INWARD TRAFFICKING CASES IN GENOVA?	58
WASTE TRAFFICKING	60
INFILTRATION IN THE LEGAL ECONOMY, CORRUPTION AND GOVERNANCE ISSUES	61
RESEARCH NOTES AND EMERGING THEMES	68

CASE STUDY 2 MELBOURNE, AUSTRALIA   71

GENERAL INFORMATION   **72**
POLICING AND SECURITY AUTHORITIES   **74**
ILLICIT TRAFFICKING   **74**
DRUG TRAFFICKING   74
WHAT ELSE CAN BE LEARNED FROM CASES OF DRUG IMPORTATIONS INTO
MELBOURNE?   80
COUNTERFEIT AND ILLICIT TOBACCO TRADE   82
OTHER ILLICIT TRADE   87
INFILTRATION IN THE LEGAL ECONOMY, CORRUPTION AND GOVERNANCE ISSUES
    90
RESEARCH NOTES AND EMERGING THEMES   **103**

CASE STUDY 3 MONTREAL, CANADA   106

GENERAL INFORMATION   **107**
POLICING AND SECURITY AUTHORITIES   **108**
ILLICIT TRAFFICKING   **109**
DRUG TRAFFICKING   109
WHAT ELSE CAN WE LEARN FROM THE DRUG TRADE AND IMPORTATION IN
MONTREAL?   115
OTHER ILLICIT TRADE   120
INFILTRATION IN THE LEGAL ECONOMY, CORRUPTION AND GOVERNANCE ISSUES
    123
RESEARCH NOTES AND EMERGING THEMES   **133**

CASE STUDY 4 NEW YORK & NEW JERSEY, USA   136

GENERAL INFORMATION	**137**
POLICING AND SECURITY AUTHORITIES	**138**
ILLICIT TRAFFICKING	**139**
DRUG TRAFFICKING	139
WHAT ELSE CAN WE LEARN FROM THE DRUG TRADE AND IMPORTATION IN NEW YORK/NEW JERSEY?	143
OTHER ILLICIT TRADE AND THE ROLE OF CBP	146
INFILTRATION IN THE LEGAL ECONOMY, CORRUPTION AND GOVERNANCE ISSUES	**151**
RESEARCH NOTES AND EMERGING THEMES	**163**

CASE STUDY 5 LIVERPOOL, UK — 168

GENERAL INFORMATION	**169**
POLICING AND SECURITY AUTHORITIES	**171**
ILLICIT TRAFFICKING	**171**
DRUG TRAFFICKING	171
WHAT ELSE CAN WE LEARN FROM/ABOUT ILLICIT TRAFFICKING AND TRADE IN LIVERPOOL?	178
INFILTRATION IN THE LEGAL ECONOMY, CORRUPTION AND GOVERNANCE ISSUES	**181**
PEEL PORT AND PORT ECONOMICS	181
FREEPORTS POST-BREXIT	184
RESEARCH NOTES AND EMERGING THEMES	**188**

LESSONS LEARNED, CHALLENGES & RECOMMENDATIONS — 192

ILLICIT TRAFFICKING	**192**
CORRUPTION	**197**

INFILTRATION IN THE LEGAL ECONOMY AND GOVERNANCE ISSUES	**200**

INTERVENING FACTORS 205

BREXIT – PRELIMINARY FORECAST	**205**
COVID-19 PANDEMIC – PRELIMINARY FORECAST	**211**
DRUG TRADE	215
CORRUPTION & INFILTRATION	219

FURTHER READING 222

BACK COVER MATTERS 229

The Research Project

Secur.Ports
Opportunities and Vulnerabilities for Organised Crime in Seaports
2019-2020

Principal Investigator
Dr Anna Sergi, Senior Lecturer (Associate Professor) in Criminology, University of Essex, UK, asergi@essex.ac.uk

Co-Investigator
Dr Luca Storti, Associate Professor in Economic Sociology, University of Turin, Italy (for New York/New Jersey), luca.storti@unito.it

Summary

This project involved **qualitative** primary research into criminality within seaports, by observing how ports, as microcosmic realities run through formal and informal relationships and have specific security vulnerabilities, which facilitate different types of illegal or deviant behaviours. Research has been carried out in two European ports (Liverpool and Genoa) and three non-European ones (Montreal, New York and Melbourne), which are either targets of, or transit zones for, criminal activities and criminal networks.

The main aim of this comparative research project was to improve policy understanding of how the complex relationships within ports act as conduits or facilitators in how criminal networks operate in the territory of and around the ports. With specific attention to the changing geopolitical conditions surrounding the port of Liverpool within the Brexit scenario, the study has looked at what could be learned in the British experience from international ones both in terms of security and in terms of transnational risk assessments.

The Project

The project has run from January 2019 to May 2020 and involved **field visits** to the various ports in this order: Genova, January-February 2019; Melbourne, March 2019; Montreal, June-July 2019; New York/New Jersey, May 2019 and August 2019; Liverpool, ad hoc visits in December 2019 and January 2020. This order is maintained in the report.

In these ports, only **container terminals** were included in the project, with the main focus remaining on large-scale trafficking through cargo.

The aim was to explore five key research questions:

1. How are informalities and vulnerabilities manifested in ports?
2. What are the perceptions and the knowledge of law enforcement and authorities on the vulnerabilities to

organised crime in ports, within the areas and regions of reference?
3. What are the aims, in the short, medium and long terms, of organised crime infiltration and mechanisms of control of the ports?
4. Is there any difference in the way criminal groups involved in similar trades behave in different ports across the same region, and, if so, what explains the differences?
5. What are the best practices and the lessons learned in detecting the infiltration of organised crime groups in port and in countering their penetration in the area?

The project involved collecting court data through national databases (through portals like Westlaw, DeIure, Pacer, Canlii, Austlii etc) but also press releases from law enforcement authorities. Interviews included port authorities, waterfront commissions, police forces, special prosecutors, and security firms working at the ports (see a list of participant institutions in the sections dedicated to each port).

Where possible a tour of the port terminals to observe the spaces directly was carried out. All data was used to contribute to academic publications in the form of journal articles and in the form of this technical report that all participants will receive.

Funding

The research is funded by The British Academy (a registered charity) under the funding call "Tackling the UK's International Challenges 2018".
Please see https://www.thebritishacademy.ac.uk for further details.

Keywords
Informality; corruption; organized crime; mafia; drug trafficking; trafficking; smuggling; border control.

Disclaimer

The report will bring the main considerations, results and findings from the ports visited in order of visit. This means that the findings will be presented as **incremental knowledge** from one port to the other; lessons learned and questions asked in one port might not have been asked in another port, as considered not relevant for that specific reality. Much depends not only on the specificity of each port, but also on the availability of data that authorities are willing to share.

This research is an exploration of the field of organised crime in seaports. Being that as it may, this report cannot provide with commentary of statistics or with exact measurements of the presence of organised crime groups and their traffics in the ports selected, but rather aims at stimulating a reflection within an analytical framework that uses different data and different qualitative resources.

This report does not give neither a comprehensive nor a complete guide to the ports, nor the quintessential truth about criminal activities in the port. Rather, it aims at bringing forward certain topics that are not often looked at together, with a view to stimulate further research.

Executive Summary – At a glance

	Top Best practice	**Top Challenge**
Genova, Italy	Port is investigated as both **a border zone and a specialist business space**. Organised crime in the port is investigated through the lenses of Antimafia tools. Partnerships across different police forces and Antimafia prosecutorial teams allow for a comprehensive approach to the phenomenon, from illicit trafficking to corruption and infiltration in the legal economy.	The urban nature of two of three container terminals and the distance of the remaining, but larger, terminal, lead to **visible variations in both security protocols as well as space governance** from authorities.

Melbourne, Australia	A very strong **local police practice, with a dedicated port taskforce**, and strong local partnerships, allow for outstanding knowledge of the territory of the port, within the urban space.	The attractiveness of Australia as an island is magnified in the **variety of smuggling methods** to bring illicit goods on the shores, including Victoria. Federal agencies, i.e. ABF and AFP, could be more involved not only in collating cross-border criminal intelligence but also in strategizing with national partners on anti-corruption in large ports.
Montreal, Canada	**Port is treated as both a transnational space and an urban one.** An embedded and dedicated federal police team allows for overarching investigations into transnational trafficking; anti-	The existence of **three levels of policing** – city, province and federal - might lead to overlapping of jurisdictions and duplication of efforts, especially for what concerns drug

	corruption units in the city and the province allow for a strong anti-infiltration focus also within the port.	trafficking, importation and distribution. The peculiar
New York/New Jersey, USA	**The port is both a gate and a governance space.** On one side, attention to outbound trafficking is a unique feature in the USA. On the other side, attention to criminality of the waterfront has historical roots (i.e. the existence and resilience of the Waterfront Commission), which allow for a specialised approach to corruption and infiltration of organised crime in the port.	**The territory of the NY/NJ port is too dispersed.** This dispersion mirrors in the duplicity of jurisdictions (the port is over two states) and in the difficult management of authorities that can deal with that duplicity. The politicisation of matters related to the port economy (from union relations to port administration businesses) leads to repeated conflicts

		and voids of governance.
Liverpool, UK	**The port is an opportunity for change.** From changing the reputation of the port and its city, to boosting the economy of the area and preparing for post-Brexit changes, the port of Liverpool is an entity that, also due to its private nature, favours efficiency and effective change.	**The port is private territory.** The public-private relationship between private port owners and public policing authorities leads to gaps in information and intelligence sharing. A multitude of voices share informed opinions on Liverpool but data is lacking. This is going to be even more challenging post-Brexit.

Table 1: Two takeaway points for each port

*****

	Emerging Convergences	**Emerging Divergences**
Illicit trafficking	- Prioritisation of investigations on drug trafficking as high harm/high gain kind of illicit trade; - Low harm/high gain types of trade (i.e. waste trafficking and contraband of tobacco) or low harm/low gain types of trade (i.e. counterfeit/contraband and of fashion goods) are lower in priority list due to resourcing. - Outbound trafficking is largely left to random controls and highly under-investigated.	- After drug trafficking, other illicit trades vary depending on location (tobacco, luxury fashion, food etc.) - Smuggling methods might vary. - Ethnic compositions of criminal networks as well as routes of illicit trade vary depending on location.

| | | | - Composition of investigation teams also vary depending on location.
- The role of Border Agencies, in between a duty and excise agency and an enforcement agency also varies depending on jurisdiction. |
|---|---|---|---|
| **Corruption** | | - Individual corruption is considered key to criminality on the waterfront, both as | - Ways to deal with these forms of corruption |

| | | an enabler of illicit trades and as a stand-alone practice.
- Corruption of dock workers is indicated as the most common factor of persistent criminality on the waterfront;
- Corruption of government agents and port employees, including border agents and terminals' employees are also persistent factors. | are extremely varied; in some cases, corruption is part of organised crime investigations while in some other cases, corruption remains a matter of public trust and therefore managed individually by different authorities.
- Systemic forms of |

		corruption are hinted by some but difficult to prove in various cases.
Infiltration & Informal Governance	- Infiltration in the port economy emerges in all ports, albeit with different impact. - At the local level, the port economy is vulnerable to infiltration in terms of contracts for construction, security, logistics (including warehousing) and transport. - At the global level, the port economy is a rather small field, whose governance is, intuitively, informal among	- Port authorities struggle with infiltration and attempts to distort governance in the port management, the more they are close to political power. - Port-city relationship apply to organised

| | | very few big players. | crime scenarios. Activities of infiltration and attempts to govern the port space vary depending on the nature, the level of sophistication and the amount of investment that organised crime groups have in the city. |

Table 2: Main terms of comparison across ports

Organised crime and the waterfront: an introduction

Popular culture is filled with images of crime on the waterfront as a business for corrupt and greedy port workers. **Historically** 'organised crime' has found a way from Melbourne to New York, from Liverpool to Montreal, to infiltrate, control and take advantage of the dockers' proximity to the ships. These inroads served the handling of the most disparate activities: from smuggling to theft, from trafficking to corruption.

Investigations run by national and international police forces, private security firms or researchers confirm that many large seaports are **hotspots** for drug trafficking and smuggling of other illegal goods; obviously size, weight and risk determine the choice of logistic channels, especially when it comes to drugs. Some institutions also point out how specialised police forces are needed as *"maritime shipments pose the greatest problem because large quantities can be transported at any one time"*[2].

Indeed, ports are unique environments; they are universes of processes and meanings. Ports are border zones, liminal areas across different juridical systems. Even morphologically they are in flux, being places of arrival and places of transit and departures, in between economic processes and political decisions. Clearly, the port is an analytical locus in

---

[2] EMCDDA and Europol, EU Drug Markets Report 2016. The Hague, 2016, page 20

which **several dilemmas of contemporary societies converge**. For example: deregulation of international trades, everyday life globalisation, endogenous tension between territories and economic escapes, illegality in markets *etc*. Ports are indeed places raising classical sociological and economic issues: the extent to which legal, grey or informal and outright criminal activities are intertwined with relations of logistics, production and management routines. Together they form the channel through which the illegal economy runs, often on the same track as that of international economic exchanges.

Ports are virtually always mentioned as key entry points for **drugs and other illegal goods,** but also as areas of influence of more sophisticated groups, who aim at governing spaces and not just profiting from them, such as mafia-type groups. In organised crime studies, deviance and crime in ports range from occasional corruption of port-workers to the employment of longshoremen on the criminal network's payroll for the purposes of continuous drug trade; port criminality might also involve the control of longshoremen's trade unions and associations and corruption of large companies involved in port administration.

The **diversification of criminal activities in a port** – more or less linked to organised crime activities and specifically to illicit trafficking – ranges from local to global and calls for a diversification of policing techniques and authorities. The port is usually public land, and might be either federal or national – at times municipal – while private actors are usually leasing the land ("landlord ports") or managing it. Indeed, **crime control** on the waterfront is a formidable task because ports are places in constant flow, with different infrastructures belonging to different owners and a multitude of authorities with jurisdictions over various aspects of port life, from economic needs and requirements to security preparedness. Various institutions have their spot in ports, from port police forces to city police agencies, from private security firms to federal/national institutions, from fire service to medical emergency. The **security and policing landscape**s of ports is built on multi-agency cooperation, as the natural answer to the challenging task that is policing the waterfront. Coordination between local law enforcement and state/federal units is challenging. The former treats the port as an urban territory and might police it as such, the latter usually see the waterfront as a border zone and thus treat it within mandates of national security and state revenues. This is especially true for customs, who, as a **hybrid** institution between administrative duties and law enforcement capacities are stretched out in their ability to monitor the port.

The characterisation of policing activities in seaports within the mandates of national security also mirrors in the **securitisation of the threat of organised crime** that has been on-going since the 1990s and even more so after 9/11, which is today central to any western state's political agenda. The **term 'organised crime'** is an umbrella term without strict boundaries. It intends to cover a number of different illegal activities from trafficking and smuggling – of drugs, weapons, human beings, counterfeit products, protected wildlife – to laundering of money. The latter covers the whole upperworld economy and finances. Violence and high-level corruption by OC may threaten the rule of law. Especially since the 2000 UN convention on Transnational Organised Crime was signed in Palermo, understanding the social and economic underpinnings of organised crime has been a priority for research to push the international community to refine definitions and abandon an Americanisation of the concept. Organised crime research is extremely wide, and if we consider the port economy as one of many economic opportunities for organised crime groups to exploit, then we can look at studies on organised crime and infiltration in different legal sectors and industries at research on money laundering and organisational crimes, and even to political and public sector corruption and investment.

Research that looks at the way organised crime groups need and use ports for their activities focuses largely on **large scale drug trafficking and importation** as much as other **forms of illegal smuggling and contraband**, such as weapons or tobacco. Transport systems in general have been often connected to illicit trades, but also to illicit governance, systemic corruption and infiltration of the port economy and management, *i.e.* infiltration of labour unions of port workers. On the one hand, because **securing borders** against illicit trade of people and goods remains one of the top priorities of the international community, effective policing and security in seaports are crucial of any strategic effort. On the other hand, ports are also extremely linked to **urban development** and urban lives. In fact, on one side there is a link between the flourishing of ports and the arrival and settlement of migrant communities, thus the changing geography of the city. On the other side, and also from a perspective of studies on organised crime, some port cities have also been sites where organised crime groups have formed and grown, as the maritime industry and economy represents a lucrative business to launder and invest proceeds. This urban perspective also encompasses questioning *to what extent* the city and the port share manifestations and evolution of organised crime activities and groups. Overall it is clear that a number of disciplines and perspectives contribute to the making of research on organised crime and the waterfront, especially from a social science perspective.

Selected Bibliography:

Abadinsky, H. *Organized Crime*, Chicago: Nelson-Hall, 1994

Beare, ME. *Transnational organized crime,* Farnham: Ashgate, 2013.

Blakey, GR and R. Goldstock, On the Waterfront": RICO and Labor Racketeering. *Scholarly Works. Paper 23.* Available for download at: http://scholarship.law.nd.edu/law_faculty_scholarship/23, 1980.

Brewer, R., *Policing the Waterfront. Networks, Partnerships and the Governance of Port Security,* Oxford: Oxford University Press, 2014.

Demeri, MJ., The 'watchdog' agency: fighting organized crime on the waterfront of New York and New Jersey. *New England Journal on Criminal and Civil Confinement* 38: 257–279, 2012.

EMCDDA and Europol, *Cocaine: A European Union perspective in the global contex.* The Hague, 2010.

EMCDDA and Europol, *EU Drug Markets Report 2016.* The Hague, 2016.

Eski, Y., *Policing, Port security and crime control. An ethnography of the port securityscape,* New York: Routledge, 2016.

Eski, Y., Customer is king: promoting port policing, supporting hypercommercialism. *Policing and Society* DOI: 10.1080/10439463.2019.1606808, 2019.

Eski, Y and R. Bujit, Dockers in drugs: policing the illegal drug trade and port employee corruption in the port of Rotterdam. *Policing: A Journal for Policy and Practice* 11(4): 371-386, 2016.

Eski, Y. and Carpenter, A., Policing in EU seaports: Impact of the ISPS code on port security post-9/11. In: M. O'Neill, K. Swinton and A. Winter (eds.) *New challenges for the EU internal security strategy* Newcastle upon Tyne: Cambridge Scholars Publishing, 71-95, 2013.

Gilliland, J., Muddy shore to modern port: redimensioning the Montreal waterfront time-space. *The*

Canadian Geographer / Le Geographe canadien 48(4): 448–472, 2004.

Jacobs, JB., *Mobsters, unions, and feds: the Mafia and the American labor movement,* New York ; London: New York University Press, 2006.

Jacobs, JB, Is labor union corruption special? *New York University Public Law and Legal Theory Working Papers* Paper 449, 2014.

Madsen, C., Pacific Gateway: state surveillance and interdiction of criminal activity on Vancouver's Waterfront. *Salus Journal* 6(1): 26-43, 2018.

Mah, A., *Port cities and global legacies. Urban identity, Waterfront work and radicalism,* London: Palgrave Macmillan, 2014.

Nordstrom, C., *Global outlaws: crime, money, and power in the contemporary world,* Berkeley; London: University of California Press, 2007.

Presidia Security Consulting, Economic sectors vulnerable to organized crime: marine port operations. Prepared for Research and National Coordination Organized Crime Division Law Enforcement and Policing Branch Public Safety Canada, Ottawa, 2011.

Sergi, A. (2020), Policing the Port, Watching the City. Manifestations of Organised Crime in the Port of Genoa, *Policing & Society: An International Journal of Research and Policy,* Online First, https://doi.org/10.1080/10439463.2020.1758103

Sergi A. (2020), Playing Pac-Man in Portville: Policing the Fragmentation and Dilution of Drug Importations through Major

Seaports, *European Journal of Criminology*, Online First, https://doi.org/10.1177/1477370820913465

Thachuk, K.L., *Transnational threats: smuggling and trafficking in arms, drugs, and human life,* Westport, Conn.: Praeger Security International, 2007.

Van Dijck, M., *Cigarette shuffle: Organising tobacco tax evasion in the Netherlands*. In P.C. van Duyne and G.A. Antonopoulos (Eds.), The Criminal Smoke of Tobacco Policy Making: Cigarette Smuggling in Europe. Nijmegen: Wolf Legal Publishers, 2009.

Von Lampe, K., *Organized crime. Analyzing illegal activities, criminal structures, and extra-legal governance,* New York: SAGE, 2016

Vujović, S., Cigarette smuggling at the local level through smugglers' eyes: How and Why?, in Van Duyne P et al (ed) The relativity of wrongdoing: Corruption, organised crime, fraud and money laundering in perspective, Oisterwijck: Wolf Legal Publishers, 2015.

Zaitch, D., From Cali to Rotterdam: perceptions of Colombian cocaine traffickers on the Dutch port. *Crime, Law and Social Change* 38(3): 239-266, 2002a.

Zaitch, D., *Trafficking cocaine: Colombian drug entrepreneurs in the Netherlands,* The Hague; London: Kluwer Law International, 2002b.

Overview: port economy and maritime security

Since the second half of the XX century, free flowing international trade has been carried predominantly by oceans and seas. World trade has been facilitated by two interconnected drivers:

1. **Policies for trade liberalisation**; decreased trading barriers and reduced tariffs have facilitated the development of an interconnected and globalised economy. Port economy is probably the best example of such a globalised economy.
2. **Reductions in transportation costs**; containerisation in particular, since after the Second World War, has significantly benefitted bilateral trade at the aggregate product level; it has increased trade flows by 75% to 100% and it has also affected positively North-South and North-North trade[3].

The business community has clearly responded to the new trading environment by increasing partnerships, and incrementing the interrelations between suppliers and consumers/customers worldwide. Indeed, as also the means, processes and volumes of production have changed and lean

---

[3] Bernhofen, Daniel M., El-Sahlid, Zouheir and Richard Kneller, Estimating the effects of containerization on world trade, Journal of International Economics, Volume 98, January 2016, Pages 36-50

towards more and more proficient and cost-efficient international transport, it is clear that the current model for growth at the global level relies on effective and conflict-free trade.

Currently, containers are the main agents of the internal and international logistics system, even though, in recent years *"weak global growth and the saturation of container diffusion continue to weigh on the growth of port volumes"*[4]. Clear **advantages of containerisation for in international trade** are[5]:

I. Standardisation of transport;
II. Flexibility of usage;
III. Computerised tracking management;
IV. Lower transport costs;
V. Warehousing;
VI. Security (as containers could in theory only be opened at the origin, destination, or for checks by customs).

In the past ten years **pressures on containerisation** have led to some **inefficiencies**. These are connected to high level of competition, the needs to invest in infrastructure and technology, and the rapid growth in the size of container ships.

---

[4] Sanchez, R.J. and Barleta, Eliana P. Reflections on the future of container ports in view of the new containerization behavior, PortEconomics Discussion Report No 3, January 2019, page 5

[5] Rodrigue, J. P., C. Comtois and B. Slack, *The Geography of Transport Systems,* Abingdon, Routledge, 2006

Shipping companies have had to rationalise their operations and are constantly driven to renovate infrastructures, reduce timings of shipment, loading and offloading, and generally work more efficiently.

Container ports are multiple-user ports, which means that no one cargo owner has a monopoly of trade. The throughput is measured by the number of TEUs[6] that the container port handles. Cargo obviously has multiple owners while shipping lines might choose dedicated terminals to call into in the different container ports. It is also worth remembering that dry bulk and other liquids might be eventually operated and owned by the same company that also owns the cargo (i.e. a company might own the extraction mine, the railway, the processing plant and the port facility at the same time).

Looking at the **organisation and the development of international terminal operators**, large conglomerates – such as APM Terminals, DP World, Cosco, PSA International, Hutchison Port Holdings Trust and the likes - are clearly dominating the economy. Some of these large conglomerates are more geographically specific, such as Hutchison Port Holdings Trust,

---

[6] The twenty-foot equivalent unit (often TEU or teu) is an inexact unit of cargo capacity often used to describe the capacity of container ships or terminals. It is based on the volume of a 20-foot-long (6.1 m) intermodal container, the standard-sized metal box which can be easily transferred between different modes of transportation, such as ships, trains and trucks (Wikipedia).

whose presence is mostly confined to China and Hong Kong even though it remains one of the largest terminal operators in the world. Others, such as PSA International – consistently the largest terminal operator – has terminals in three continents and 16 countries, but not Australia, nor Africa nor North America. APM Terminals has presence in 39 countries, DP world, with over 65 terminals, spans over 6 continents.

With such global economy and the challenges of global markets, the port economy is clearly a very profitable and also a very competitive field. **Performance** of ports and container terminals depends on many different factors including but not limited to intra-port competition across several terminal operators. Other factors include port access channel and land-side access, the quality of backhaul area, the type of cargo handling equipment, the nature of labour and trade relations, and also the efficiency of custom, police and security checks.

Predictably, the landscape of **maritime security** has changed drastically together with all the security measures in other fields after the events of 9/11. This created a drive to securing borders and ensuring the safety of citizens and of infrastructures have become the main challenges of today's world. The new drive to security had a broad effect on the maritime institutions.

The International Maritime Organisation (IMO) in 2002 approved the **International Ship and Port Facility Security (ISPS) Code** by adding Chapter XI.2 (Special measures to enhance maritime security) to the SOLAS (Safety of Life at Sea) Convention of 1974. These provisions marked an increasingly neat difference between safety and security in the maritime field.

- **Maritime Safety** refers to the development of emergency and contingency planning concerned with the prevention of accidental damage or incidents to marine environments or loss of life at sea.
- **Maritime Security** refers to measures aimed at preventing intentional damage through sabotage, subversion, or other maritime threats, such as use of force or threats to territorial sovereignty; terrorist acts against ships and ports; piracy and armed robbery at sea; transnational organised crime such as smuggling or trafficking; illegal, unregulated and unreported (IUU) fishing; environmental threats, i.e. illegal dumping.

The addition of Chapter XI became broadly accepted: in mid-2020, the ISPS applies to 165 SOLAS members accounting for over 99% of world tonnage. The Code contains a mandatory **Part A** that outlines detailed maritime and port security-related requirements, which SOLAS contracting governments, port authorities and shipping companies must adhere to. **Part B** of the Code provides a series of recommendatory guidelines on how to meet the requirements of Part A. Part A of details mandatory measures to be taken by contracting governments, shipowners, and ports while part B lists voluntary measures to enhance maritime security. Certainly, as ports are gateways and marine borders and therefore are crucial in any strategic effort to secure transit, entry in, and exit out of states, maritime security has been developing along the lines of the policing of other security threats, including terrorism and organised crime, especially illicit trafficking of drugs.

Beyond the compulsory elements of the **IMO package** are mandatory national initiatives, binding vessels and cargos to extra measures when passing through certain waters. Most states have supplemental rules to the IMO package, as, for example, the United States has interpreted the recommendations in part B of the ISPS code as being mandatory for American-bound vessels since the beginning[7].

The **measures prescribed in SOLAS XI and the ISPS Code** can be broadly broken down into **five** major categories according to their focus. These are:

I. *Measures targeting contracting governments*. These include, among other things, determining and set security levels (e.g. 1=low, 2=medium and 3=high); determining which port facilities are required to designate a Port Facility Security Officer; ensuring completion and approval of a Port Facility Security Assessment and the Port Facility Security Plan for each

---

[7] OCDE, Security In Maritime Transport: Risk Factors And Economic Impact Maritime Transport Committee, July 2003

port facility that serves ships engaged on international voyages; communicating with IMO.

II. ***Measures targeting ships.*** These include three ship-related provisions: the equipment of Automatic Identification Systems (AIS); the permanent marking and display of the ship's unique identification number; the installation of a ship security alert system.

III. ***Measures targeting maritime carrier companies.*** These include designating of a Company Security Officer (CSO); undertaking a Ship Security Assessment (SSA); Developing a Flag-State-approved Ship Security Plan (SSP); Designating a Ship Security Officer (SSO); generally ensuring adequate training to carry out security provisions as approved and appropriate.

IV. ***Measures targeting ports.*** These include: approving and carrying out port facility security assessments; developing port facility security plans to respond to security alert levels; designate a Port Facility Security Officer (PFSO) and carry out adequate training for security personnel.

V. ***Other certification/documentary requirements.*** These include notifications of arrival; manifest rules; visa requirements.

Organised crime in ports: trafficking, corruption and governance

For the purposes of this report **organised crime** refers to complex, multi-layered and usually serious criminalised activity that is aimed at both **profit accumulation or reinvestment** (in the form of trafficking, illicit trade and infiltration in the legal economy) and at **power grabbing** (in the form of acquisition of contracts, and in general of financial, political and administrative power)[8]. In line with this working definition, organised crime in ports includes **complex activities** such as illicit trafficking, illicit trade, money laundering and/or infiltration in the legal economy, as much as **behaviours** of corruption: both as enabler of trafficking and as governance tool.

Illegal tobacco trade, the trafficking of narcotics - especially cocaine, heroin, marijuana and hashish - together with the trafficking in human beings and firearms trafficking, constitute the main complex criminal activities that go through ports on a daily basis. To this, one might want to add trafficking of cultural, stolen or looted, artefacts, wildlife trafficking, trafficking of counterfeit products, trafficking of hazardous, toxic or non-declared waste and the likes.

---

[8] Sergi, A. From Mafia to Organised Crime: A Comparison of Policing Models, New York and London: Palgrave Macmillan, 2017

Illicit Trafficking and trade through seaports are probably the obvious downsides of progress. Trade infrastructures, such as an effective seaport, may enable the economic benefits of globalisation, but at the same time will make countries and borders more vulnerable to forms of complex and organised crime engaged in illicit trafficking. **There is no trafficking route that is not already a trade route**.

Even though trade routes have been used for trafficking all sorts of licit and illicit products, trafficking of drugs remains the most profitable and the most frequent of illicit trades. According to the World Customs Organisation (WCO) and their annual Illicit Trade Report, in 2018, 126 countries submitted 45,497 drug trafficking cases to the WCO[9], among which those cases related to cannabis and cocaine trafficking constituted the majority. Especially for **cocaine**, an interesting data shared by the WCO is that although most seizures happen on cocaine trafficked by air, the overall amount seized in transit through vessels is much higher. In other words, air and mail seizures accounted for 72.7% of all cocaine seizures, although vessels were the method implicated in the most significant seizures in terms of quantity seized (146,675 kilogrammes, or 76.5% of the total)[10].

---

[9] http://www.wcoomd.org/-/media/wco/public/global/pdf/topics/enforcement-and-compliance/activities-and-programmes/illicit-trade-report/itr_2018_en.pdf?db=web
[10] Ibid., page 49

Another interesting set of data by WCO in relation to **IPR**, health and safety products (Intellectual Property Rights related to mobile phones, computers, footwear, clothing, even games and toys) shows that seizures executed on vessels made up the largest percentage in the number of pieces seized, constituting 57.3% (31,573,528) of the overall total for 2018[11]. This mirrors in data related to **contraband** of medical products seized, as seizures conducted on vessels netted the majority of contraband retrieved, responsible for 279,381,340 (80.7%) of a total 346,086,991 pieces recovered[12]. A same trend for **tobacco and alcohol**, as WCO shows that products seizures were from vehicles, even though the conveyance method accounting for the greatest number of pieces was indeed vessels. Indeed, with various types of illicit trades, the use of **maritime routes** seems to be impacting if not the number of seizures, certainly the quantity of products seized.

Whereas illicit trade and trafficking are the main manifestations of complex criminality – often but not always connected to organised crime groups – they are also mostly transit crimes. Ports are indeed either **doors** – of entry as much as exit - or **gates** – of entry, exit and transit - in trafficking activities. Trafficking is mostly detected coming inward, but occasionally outward trafficking is also of interest. While each

---

[11] Ibid., page 117
[12] Ibid., page 131

state has their own mechanisms of control and intelligence about trafficking products and routes, the international community has attempted to synchronise data collection and interventions cross-borders. For example, **the UNODC-WCO Container Control Programme (CCP)** was established as a joint initiative of the UNODC and the WCO in 2004. The program aims to provide continuous monitoring and oversight, offering a plethora of context-specific trainings and strengthening cooperation between state agencies and with the private sector. With specific attention to improving risk management and enhance security in the supply chain while also facilitating trade, the CCP is operational in over 50 countries and has over 100 Port Control Units that are supposedly equipped to exchange information, intelligence about high-risks containers and obviously facilitate seizures cross-borders.

However, beyond the efforts to track and investigate cargo through containers, most trafficking activities also include different degrees of **corruption**, as clearly getting across border security and checks and around duties, taxes and other forms of certifications requires knowledge from within and at times specialist knowledge as well.
Corruption in ports can take different forms, but specifically we can find it both in relation to trafficking **(corruption as enabling practice and/or resource)** as much as in relation to port economy and its development **(corruption as autonomous practice)** .

Corruption is also a cost for trade. Precisely for this reason, the *"Maritime Anti-Corruption Network (MACN) is a global business network working towards the vision of a maritime industry free of corruption that enables fair trade to the benefit of society at large"*[13]. With now over 100 members in the maritime companies, MACN's members have joined forces to raise awareness of the challenges of corruption; implement common Anti-Corruption principles; develop and shar best practices; collaborate with governments, non-governmental organizations, and civil society to identify and mitigate the root causes of corruption; and create and promote a culture of integrity within the maritime community. From demands for payments, to small in-kinds bribes, from non-transparent tariffs to incoherent regulations for approval of vessels, MACN has started to promote 'say no' campaigns together with ethical standards.

As the maritime industry's priority is to promote and ensure smooth business, the power that some port officials have, can clearly be distorted, corrupted, and therefore affect business, reputation, investments and trade. Specifically, **corruption at the border** is a matter difficult to discuss and to research. Clearly, border control authorities play an important role in facilitating trade and the circulation of goods and people across countries. With increasing demands for smooth global trade, borders are porous and difficult to control; corruption at

---

[13] https://www.maritime-acn.org/about-macn

the borders has a detrimental, especially linked to illicit trafficking, impacts on a country's revenue collection and business activity in addition to impacting the maritime industry. Factors that have been identified as increasing corruption risks in border regions are[14]:

    I.   Geographic dispersion, isolation and remoteness of borders;
    II.   Size and type of border configuration might affect work patterns across border guards;
    III.   Administrative monopoly and discretionary powers for border guards and customs officials;
    IV.   Salaries and working conditions can offer incentives to accept bribes;
    V.   High tariffs, non-transparent and burdensome complex regulatory frameworks;
    VI.   Pressure from organised crime groups that might result in threats, intimidation and violence.

While for trafficking activities corruption might be more or less occasional and specific (i.e. a corrupt border agent might serve a network once or repeatedly, and the same network can use different corrupt agents at once), when it comes to the port economy, corruptive behaviours often take more systemic or

---

[14] Chêne M, Transparency International, Corruption at borders, 2018, https://knowledgehub.transparency.org/assets/uploads/helpdesk/Corruption-at-borders-2018.pdf

endemic forms. For example, **'facilitation gifts'** can be negotiated by seafarers to an array of port officials in many parts of the world. Recipients ranged from health inspectors, to customs and immigration officers, and from agents and pilots, to terminal staff. The pervasiveness of this practice is staggering, as about 91% of respondents in a 2016 study involving over 2,500 active seafarers around the world, admitted to have witnessed this practice[15].

Petty corruption, exchanges of favours, unethical behaviours, nepotism, misappropriations, including heft, embezzlement, falsification of records and fraud, infiltration in the port economy and bureaucracy all cost **port governance** in terms of business, administration, revenues, security, and even health. The bureaucracy of port economies and authorities is not only extremely complex, but also competitive and fast-paced, thus making the port an ideal environment for corruption, with high gains and low detection rates. Officials in ports engage in[16]:

---

[15] Sampson H., Acejo I., Ellis N., Tang L, Turgo N. The relationships between seafarers and shore-side personnel: An outline report based on research undertaken in the period 2012-2016, Seafarers International Research Centre (SIRC) Cardiff University, 2016
https://www.sirc.cf.ac.uk/Uploads/Publications/The%20relationships%20between%20seafarers%20and%20shore-side%20personnel.pdf

[16] Sequeira, S. and Djankov, S., An Empirical Study of Corruption in Ports, London School of Economics, MPRA Paper No. 21791, 2010
https://mpra.ub.uni-muenchen.de/21791/1/MPRA_paper_21791.pdf

- **Collusive corruption**: when public officials and private agents collude to share rents generated by the illicit transaction; Collusive corruption is cost-reducing; it increases a firm's demand for the public service.
- **Coercive corruption**: when a public bureaucrat coerces a private agent into paying an additional fee, above and beyond the official price, just to gain access to the public service or good. Coercive corruption is cost-increasing; it reduces a firm's demand for the public service.

The organisational structure of different port environments creates incentives for corrupt behaviour; structural opportunities to exchange, requests, demand, accept a bribe plays an important role in the motivation for corrupt behaviour. The reduction of in-person contacts between clearing agents and officials, or the introduction of online submission of documentation for pre-clearance programs may also reduce opportunities for corruption[17]. However, illegal intrusions into port governance might not just be about authorities and their bureaucracy, as much as it is also about **patronage, administrative and political corruption** inside and outside of port authorities and economy (including corruption of industry relations agents and partners and election/nominations of management roles).

---

[17] Ibid.

Administrative corruption in port can take different forms, such as manipulation of procurement tenders, extracting kickbacks from service operators in the border area and appointment or promotion of officers based on nepotism. It usually involves the participation of higher levels of management or leadership in the authority[18]. **Political patronage and other power-grabbing forms of corruption** can manifest as attempts to amend regulations to serve interests of certain groups, people, or companies. In some cases, private companies might unduly influence border authorities, senior management or other individuals/actors who can have a say in approving security provisions and specific regulations for the port. When senior management in the port authority and/or high-ranking staff in border agencies have political links, appointments might be considered as either rewards or disapproval for political support or lack of it[19]. In other cases, complex corruption networks may involve local businesses engaged in the cross-border trafficking of goods and local politicians that benefit from associating with them for their political career.

---

[18] Center for the Study of Democracy, Study on Anti-Corruption Measures in EU Border Control, 2012
http://www.frontex.europa.eu/assets/publications/research/study_on_anticorruption_measures_in_e u_border_control.pdf

[19] Chêne, 2018, op.cit; Center for the Study of Democracy, 2012, op.cit.

Case Study 1
Genova, Italy

Photo: SECH Terminal, February 2019, Author's rights

General Information

The port of Genova is Italy's biggest port. Since 2016[20] it includes four different port realities: Genova, Prà, Vado Ligure and Savona, as the Western Ligurian Sea Port Authority. This project only focused on **Genova and Prà container terminals** as it occurred before the unification of the ports under the same authority took place.

The port ranks 68th in the world's largest container ports and 8th in Europe[21]. With a total of 30 terminals, of which 6 container terminals, and a total of 2.7 million TEUs of container traffic per year, the amounts of goods and passengers going through Genova is impressive. With 22 km of waterfront and 7 million square meters, as a **landlord port**, Genova's port public land is leased out (law 84/1994) to private companies who run the port facility's economic activities as well as implement security regulations by nominating a Port Facility Security Office (PFSO) as required by the ISPS code. Around 30,000 people work at the Port of Genova, says its website.

The **main terminals for containers** - Terminal PSA Voltri Prà (until May 2019 known as Voltri Terminal Europe, VTE, or simply Voltri), Terminal Sech (South European Container Hub),

---

[20] Legislative Decree no.169/2016 unifying the port authorities of Genova and Savona ports.
[21] One Hundred Ports 2018 - Lloyd's List Maritime Intelligence Informa - https://lloydslist.maritimeintelligence.informa.com/one-hundred-container-ports-2018

Spinelli Group Terminal, Calata Bettolo MSC Terminal (launched in March 2019), Intermodal Marine Terminal (until 2016 Terminal Messina) and Terminal San Giorgio – operate mainly with traders from China, United States, and Singapore, in over 450 ports across the world and being the last port of call on the Far East-Mediterranean maritime trade routes. The port has natural deep water - that requires no dredging minimal tidal range and favourable marine weather conditions – and offers as well a variety of intra-Med, feeder and ro-ro service. Thanks to its strategic geographical location – it's located at the most northern point of the Mediterranean Sea – this port provides easy access Northern Italy and Southern Europe. Through a well-connected motorway network and direct rail connections to the Genova-Rotterdam Corridor (still in its final stage of development), the logistics chain operating in the Genova ports, is aimed at increasing effective and prompt movements of goods across the region.

Police and Security Authorities

During the course of the project, a total of 12 meetings were held, in the form of collective interviews, focus groups and individual interviews with: Capitaneria di Porto (port authority security office), Direzione Distrettuale Antimafia (DDA, district antimafia prosecutor office), Procura della Repubblica (public prosecutor office), Guardia di Finanza (fiscal police), Polizia di Frontiera (border police), Agenzia delle Dogane e dei Monopoli (customs and revenue agency), Direzione Investigativa Antimafia (DIA, investigative antimafia directorate) in the Genoa province. Also, access to three container terminals, SECH, Spinelli and Voltri (now PSA Genova Prà) was granted and also included conversations with the three Port Facility Security Officers (PFSOs) there.

Illicit trafficking

Drug trafficking

In the last years, Guardia di Finanza and Antimafia prosecutors (DDA) in Genova, together with the dell'Agenzia delle Dogane e Monopoli (customs and revenues) have completed various operations against drug trafficking in the port of Genova. In particular, in Genova, 'ndrangheta clans (groups linked or belonging to the Calabrian mafia) seem to be active in the port for trafficking of cocaine from South America. Increased seizures of heroin from Afghanistan specifically (overall 28,35% of heroin seized in Italy was seized in the region of Liguria in 2018[22]) demonstrate the rising role of the port in the trafficking of this commodity as well.

---

[22] Prefettura - Ufficio Territoriale del Governo di Genova - Comunicato Stampa Conferenza Regionale Delle Autorita' Di Pubblica Sicurezza 6 August 2019, Sistema portuale ligure – prevenzione e contrasto delle attività illecite - https://www.interno.gov.it/sites/default/files/allegati/ ge_conferenza_regionale_autorita_pubblica_sicurezza.pdf

Operation Artabaz, in 2018, is a perfect example of the work done by the authorities in coordination with others, in their attempt to curb both heroin and cocaine trafficking. The seizure of around 270 kgs of heroin on board of the ship Artabaz in November 2018 has marked the largest heroin seizure in the past 20 years, for a total value of over 10 million euros. The ship had left the Iranian port of Bandar Abbas, headed towards Turkey and in Europe calling at Hamburg, Valencia and Genova, where 31 containers were offloaded in Terminal Spinelli. Three of these containers contained the heroin, camouflaged among bags of bentonite (materials for construction). Further 2 kgs of the drug were left to proceed by truck, in a controlled shipment that was meant to lead to the arrests of whoever was behind it. In practice, the investigation had started from Belgium the summer before – the drug seized in Genova was the second shipment that traffickers could not send to Antwerp in that occasion as there they knew they were controlled there. Belgian police had sent authorities in Genova all the necessary information to intercept the containers and had agreed with them the controlled shipment under the European Investigative Order. Authorities didn't know what as the final destination of the drug. The buyer linked to those containers – in this case a man linked to a company based in Czech Republic – had to contact the shipping agent (in Austria) with further details on how to deliver the shipment; the man was in fact very preoccupied to clarify which container went where and how. The final address was in Rosendhal, in the Netherlands, but very close to Antwerp, were two arrests were finally made. Neither the shipping agent nor the truck driver knew anything about the drugs in the container.

Another case, coded **Operation 'Buon Vento Genovese'** (Good Genoan Wind), in summer 2019, led to the arrest of three Italian citizens for international drug trafficking from South America, with the aggravating factor of the mafia method and presence. In this case, the network was part of the 'ndrina (clan) Alvaro, a mafia group from the Calabrian 'ndrangheta in Sinopoli (Reggio Calabria). Antonio Alvaro was intercepted in Bogotà, Colombia while buying large quantities of cocaine. In this case the authorities in Genova worked with Eurojust, Colombian authorities, the DEA (Drug Enforcement Administartion) and the CBP (Customs and Border Protection) in the USA. In Genova, **368 kgs of cocaine**, worth about 100 million euros, at high level of purity, led to the arrest of said Antonio Alvaro in Colombia, Domenico Romeo, also linked to the same 'ndrina and for a long time a fugitive too, and other two men, Rodolfo Militano and Filippo Ierinò based between Calabria and Liguria. Alvaro's brother Vincenzo had already been arrested in an anti-drug operation in 2014, codenamed **Operation Docks**, involving personnel from then VTE (now PSA Genova Prà) terminal. The 2019 operation, that also led to the seizure of 3 cars, cash for a total value of about 950,000 euros, various encrypted phones and a jammer to prevent radio-transmitting, confirms the trend that sees the 'ndrangheta as a major player in cocaine trafficking and provision in Italy and abroad (see also Operation Papas and

Panda, in 2015). Furthermore, **Operation Rebuffo**, in 2017 and **Operation Chiamata** in 2019, have confirmed some trends in cocaine importations in Genova. These operations have in common the same broker, Massimo Rocca, port worker with the CULMV[23] in Spinelli Terminal, convicted in 2018 for Operation Rebuffo. In the first case, the network, which had links with Albanian individuals based in Northern Italy, used the **rip-on rip-off system** of placing bags full of cocaine bricks or bags at the doors of the container, easily taken out in the port once arrived. In the second case, which involved direct contacts with suppliers in Latin America (Colombia), the network was heavily relying on information on dates and specific locations of arrival of containers in the terminal given to and by some port workers, among which Rocca, so that the drug could be offloaded and then distributed. The importer in this case, a small entrepreneur from Genova, had alleged links with a 'ndrangheta clan as well.

When it comes to drug shipments where 'ndrangheta or other mafia clans are involved, apart from what eventually makes it to a courtroom for a trial, intelligence is much richer, as antimafia operations are more permissive and more intrusive. From **mafia investigations**, authorities have learned the

---

[23] The Compagnia Unica (The Unified Company)– or more specifically the Compagnia Unica fra i Lavoratori delle Merci Varie (CULMV) (The Unified Company for Workers of Various Commodities) – is the main and the most historically relevant service company active in the port of Genova. Its members are also known as 'camalli'. The CULMV refused to be involved in the research project.

following, specifically applicable to **cocaine** and the port of Genova.
   a. Port workers and employees know who they are dealing with when mafia members are involved, as they tend to **intimidate** workers and their families.
   b. In cross-border shipments, the **person of reference** is usually a mafia/'ndrangheta affiliate, as it's a matter of reputation and guarantee.
   c. There are mechanisms in place **to control the quality of cocaine** that gets shipped is the same of that which arrives. These might include using stamps, barcodes, pictures of the seals with phones only used to do that and so on. These experiments also serve the purpose to understand who to trust in the team available.
   d. A usual way to structure the cocaine job, in addition to the rip-on rip-off system is the employment of a **front shipment** – that diverts the attention of authorities onto a smaller shipment while the bigger one goes somewhere else undetected. When front shipments are used, the control mechanisms is operated from the territories above Liguria, in the **southern part of Piemonte**, where the 'ndrangheta clans are territorially stronger and can better support coordination.

Other illicit trade

Even though, according to Customs, the trade of **counterfeit products** is in decline, the port remains a hub for such illicit trade due to the prominence of shipping routes from China and India, where most of counterfeit products come from. In particular, the following trends make the scenario interesting:

1. Counterfeit goods or goods ready to be counterfeited come mostly from China or India, but fake labels either come from other countries, i.e. Morocco or Tunisia, or are made in/around Genova directly.
2. In an attempt to cheat duty checks, goods usually are first offloaded in other low-risk countries as, upon arriving in Genova, only the last place of transit is relevant for checks.
3. **Counterfeiting of industrial patents and brands** (intellectual property rights) are increasing, as per perceptions of customs and anti-fraud officers, as products destined to counterfeit markets are indeed processed and 'created' locally by using fake labels and counterfeit brands.

Counterfeit might also include **perishable or food** products. In Operation Provvidenza[24] in 2016, custom officers in VTE- Voltri terminal (now terminal PSA Genova Prà) intercepted around 130,000 labels for extra virgin olive oil that had been falsely declared as 'tissues and towels' destined to the USA.

---

[24] Procura della Repubblica presso il Tribunale Ordinario di Reggio Calabria- Direzione Distrettuale Antimafia - Proc. Pen. n. 206/2017 R.G.N.R. Mod. 21 DDA (stralcio del proc.pen.n. 2160/15 R.G.N.R. Mod. 21 DDA) - Fermo Di Indiziato Di Delitto.

Those labels were then used to perfect a commercial fraud, where inferior quality blended oil (imported into the US by another company, also involved in the fraud) was sold as extra-virgin olive oil from Calabria or from Tuscany. Behind this operation, that beyond the **food fraud** also involved drug trafficking through Gioia Tauro and Genova ports, was the Piromalli clan, from Gioia Tauro, one of the most prominent 'ndrangheta clans.

An interesting case of **contraband pharmaceuticals**, in 2017, investigated a shipment containing 16 tons of tramadol (24 million pills) for a value of over 50 million euros – the so-called fighters' drugs. Authorities in Genova tracked the container – labelled as transporting clothing and cosmetic products - destined to Libya. The container was loaded in India, transiting through Genova after some strange and unusual other stops, offloaded in Genova and placed on another ship destinated to the Calabrian port of Gioia Tauro. Authorities in Genova alerted the colleagues in Calabria where the cargo was seized. That one or more 'ndrangheta clans might have been working for or with terrorist cells in Libya was a strong hypothesis in this case. In general, for **counterfeit or contraband pharmaceuticals,** it's not just about the organisation of the shipment, as much as it is a matter of masking documentation to elude duty and anti-fraud checks.

What further things can we learn from inward trafficking cases in Genova?

i. There are people in the port and in the city that are considered as **being 'available'** for a variety of networks and of jobs, irrespective of ethnic origins and social status. These individuals usually hold positions in the port, as port workers or terminal employees, and usually remain 'available' for certain period of time until arrested.

ii. The structure to **open containers in the port** has to be very organised: a single port worker is not enough; there must be a way to make the crane operator place the container in a specific position; the rota of port workers must be accessible, thus access to terminals is key.

iii. After monitoring the 'available' persons for a while, authorities start seeing the subjects who act as **'trait-d'union'** with the importing network/organisation.

iv. The organisation usually becomes visible only when the drugs are *let out* of the port. This usually happens when Genova is the **final destination** for the shipment and the shipment is on the radar of authorities because it also involves locals.

v. When the drugs or other goods are intercepted in Genova but Genova was not the intended destination, importers are usually less visible and connected on the territory. This might mean that communications

vi. between parties and the management of the shipment is handled **remotely**.
vi. **Corruption** in illicit trafficking is confirmed as enabling practice (it's needed to complete the job) or as a resource (through the people made 'available', prone at being corrupted). In many recent cases the **payment** to corrupted employees or workers was made directly **with the drugs** (e.g. payment through a brick of cocaine), which poses extra problems for distribution channels.
vii. **Scanners** are not the main or most reliable tool in anti-trafficking efforts. Also, scanners are used **only upon request**. Rough figures speak of **1 out of 10,000** containers routinely checked, about **4-5%** of the total containers selected by the system for controls. It is easier to find contraband by chance in a container that looks unusual or whose cargo is unusual, than finding cocaine in a bag at the front of a container that carries precisely what it claims to be carrying.
viii. As it is increasingly difficult to open containers in the terminals – due to the **displacement effect of increased security controls** – it is more likely that the drugs leave the port with the container, which involves the transport system and the whole supply chain in the investigation and, eventually, the infiltration mechanisms. Another option is to move to another, smaller, port in the area.

Waste trafficking

While most of the attention to illicit trafficking focuses on inward trade, particular attention in Genova is paid to **outward** trafficking and in particular international waste trafficking. Illicit waste is made of waste that is not properly disposed of, or for which specific duties are not paid. Usually hidden in **containers** of furnishings, clothing, old electrical appliances or vehicles, illicit waste from Genova is routinely directed to Africa - Nigeria, Ghana, Senegal, Benin, Egypt, Cameroon, Burkina Faso, Tunisia, Togo - and also to China and India. Mostly this waste is plastic, unused or overused tyres and other rubber residuals, pieces from cars/motorbikes/trucks, batteries and vehicle compressors, gas tanks, electronic waste and clothing of various fabrics. With around 6,000 kgs of illicit waste seized in the port of Genova in 2015, 10,000 kgs in 2016, in 2017 a peak of 1,197,611 kgs has alarmed authorities, followed by 605,350 in 2018 and about 160,000 in the first half of 2019[25]. This type of trafficking is not solely meant for easy disposal at sea or in the destination country (for elusion of otherwise expensive procedures), but could also be meant for re-use elsewhere. The modus operandi usually includes a shipment registered by an individual and labelled as **'personal**

---

[25] Prefettura - Ufficio Territoriale del Governo di Genova - Comunicato Stampa Conferenza Regionale Delle Autorita' Di Pubblica Sicurezza 6 August 2019, Sistema portuale ligure – prevenzione e contrasto delle attività illecite - https://www.interno.gov.it/sites/default/files/allegati/ge_conferenza_regionale_autorita_pubblica_sicurezza.pdf

goods'. This individual is usually a third party that is used/paid to take the responsibility for the cargo.

While it appears clear that behind the lucrative trafficking of waste might be organised crime structures or at the very least **predatory white collar and corporate crime**, at the level of customs this is not easily seen. However, in 2018, the Ecologic unit of the Carabinieri in Genova (Nucleo Operativo Ecologico dei Carabinieri) has checked overall 160 companies (43 of which in Genova) and provided fines for over 45,000 euros and around 3,5 million euros in seized assets.

Infiltration in the legal economy, corruption and governance issues

The economy of the port is not only lucrative from a trade perspective, but also because of the series of services and contracts that it forges and attract. In both inbound illicit trafficking, such as drugs or counterfeit goods, and outbound ones, such as waste trafficking, the role of companies is key. Whether companies are set up as tools/means to facilitate illicit trades, or are the perpetrators of illicit activities themselves, the legal economy around **the port remains particularly porous to infiltration, enabling and autonomous forms of corruption** that invest mostly trade relationships and at times political and administrative spheres too.

Two companies, Eurotransit Italia and Eurotransit Group, with headquarters in Genova and branches in San Ferdinando, in Calabria, near the port of Gioia Tauro, have been prevented from providing services in Genova, because of an **antimafia interdiction**[26] by the Prefect of Genova. The companies in question belonged to four men, brothers and sons, Domenico, Gioacchino, Salvatore, and Massimo Careri. Eurotransit Italia had been established in 2013 while Eurotransit Group in 2018 – they both were offering services of transport (trucks, large vehiclesì, lorries for selling, or renting) and had their offices inside the Distripack building of the VTE (PSA Genova Prà) terminal. Thanks to strategic marriages, the Careri family is linked to affiliates of the Molè clan, which, together with the Piromalli clan, has mafia sovereignty in the town of Gioia Tauro in Calabria. The Careris also had other ventures, among which S.G.F Careri S.r.l., oil producers involved in the abovementioned **Operation Provvidenza**. Domenico and his son Gioacchino in fact had been already arrested for arranging the shipment of the blended olive oil destined to the USA with fake labels on behalf

---

[26] The Antimafia interdiction is defined by paragraph 3 of art. 84 of Legislative Decree no. 159/2011 and it consists of the declaration of the existence of one of the causes of revocation, suspension or prohibition referred to in article 67 – certifying the existence of any mafia infiltration attempts which could influence the choices and directions of the companies or enterprises concerned. Grounds for revocation of licenses, authorisations, concessions, registrations, certifications, qualifications and disbursements as well as the prohibition to conclude public contracts for works, services and supplies, and related subcontracting, including piecework of any type, freight and any type of supplies.

of the Piromalli clan, through the ports of Gioia Tauro and Genova. They clearly had the know-how on how to move around both ports, to avoid duties, document checks, move containers and eventually exploit the port economy.

The **transport industry** around the port is permeable to the interests of organised crime, nationally but also cross-borders – with **complacent** and proactive company managers – as in the case of Operation Provvidenza – as much as with **unaware** shipping agents, like in the case of Operation Artabaz mentioned above. A specific point was made by the Guardia di Finanza in Genova: the more security systems make it difficult to move around the terminals (and therefore to pick up illicit goods from containers) the more illicit goods will need to get out of the port, hence **control/infiltration/setting-up/exploitation** of transport companies becomes the obvious solution.

Other types of infiltration in the legal economy of the port of Genova relate to the **construction industry**. In particular, as noted by both one of the PFSO and also by the Guardia di Finanza, **space** is a real issue in the port of Genova. The city itself is compressed between the mountains and the sea, making it very difficult to expand: as put it by the PFSO of SECH terminal, *"a square meter of land in the port of Genova is gold"*. The management of space, and of construction contracts, could escalate to more **systemic or endemic forms of corruption,** to the point that corruption becomes a form of **governing the market**.

In 2015-2016 a corruption scandal in Rome invested contracts at the port of Genova too. The relevant facts, of what is a very complex case of corruption, developed as follows:

- The events relate to the construction works of the new container terminal (now, in 2020, operational) in **Calata Bettolo**, a strip of land in between Terminal SECH, Spinelli Terminal, and Terminal Rinfuse in the old port area in the city.
- One of the companies that won the contract, in mid 2000, was **Tecnis S.p.a.,** based in Catania, Sicily, one of the largest companies of the South of Italy.
- The works of Calata Bettolo underwent a series of delays until, in 2014, the Port authority, through an 'amicable settlement', added 46 million euros to the initial 140 million euros budget.
- The Public Prosecutor Office in Rome, in **Operation Dama Nera**[27] (part 1 and 2), since 2015, started investigating various cases of systemic corruption, self-laundering, trafficking of favours, and bid rigging within ANAS S.p.A[28]. Among these occurrences, many involved

---

[27] Press Office, Guardia di Finanza, http://www.gdf.gov.it/stampa/ultime-notizie/anno-2016/marzo/operazione-dama-nera-2-19-arrestati-tra-imprenditori-professionisti-dirigenti-e-funzionari-di-anas-s.p.a

[28] Formerly an acronym for Azienda Nazionale Autonoma delle Strade, (National Autonomous Roads Corporation), ANAS is an Italian government-owned company deputed to the construction and maintenance of Italian motorways.

bribes (called "cherries") that were used to feed maxi-variants, rises of costs during construction masked by amicable agreements, like the one of Calata Bettolo.
- In 2016, Tecnis is the leader company in a consortium of 24 companies that were subjected to **judiciary administration** as per preventative order of the tribunal in Catania, *following Operation Dama Nera in Rome*. The leader companies, through direct decisions of their administrators – charged with corruption - were said to contribute to mafia businesses, linked to the clan Santapaola of Cosa Nostra.
- In addition, and *de relato*, the chief engineer who managed the works for the Port Authority, Andrea Pieracci, has been sentenced to two years of imprisonment for the crime of abuse of office (art. 323 of the Italian penal code). As technical manager of the Port Authority of Genova, in 2010, in violation of the law, he provided an unjust capital advantage to companies by fragmenting a large contract into smaller contracts to avoid that could be assigned directly without the proper tender procedure[29]. He had also been charged receiving money as a private consultant from a company with whom he was also dealing with at the Port, but he has been cleared for that.

---

[29] Corte Appello di Genova, sentenza Andrea Pieracci 28.02.2017

While obviously the single judiciary positions of individuals and companies involved in this case remain a matter for the courts of law, this chain of events show the potential disruptive capacity that decision making in the Port authority entails. Another series of events invested the works of Calata Bettolo, among other construction and development works at the port. The case is one of corruption, bribery and bid rigging that since 2003 has had different manifestations and actors, according to the Court of Appeal of Genova. The Court had judged some of the most influential private sectors entrepreneurs in the port and managers of the Port authority as they essentially nourished a cartel to push away certain contractors and split the works among them, by controlling licensing and qualifications for the tenders. The Supreme Court, also evaluating the case in 2014, notices[30]:

> "The Port Authority enjoys a substantial sphere of discretional power. It is not possible to consider the existence of a public tender in the cases where potential contractors are individually invited to present their bids but the Authority remains free to choose the winner within a framework of convenience and opportunity similar to that of the private sector".

---

[30] Corte di Cassazione, Sezione Penale Sesta, Sentenza N. 32237 - 13.03.2014, page 47

Also in this case, as in the previous one, individual responsibility remains a matter for the courts to decide. There is, however, evidence of unjust favours to certain companies, abuse of power from the Port Authority managers, and lack of control over companies (such as the abovementioned CULMV) in their requirements to proceed with certain checks on their staff who worked on the port.

While in the previous case, corruption was one of the means used to infiltrate the port economy, in this case corruption was an autonomous practice, and this effectively could alter the **governance** of the port authority and the port developments. Individuals in power managed to direct tenders and bids affecting the port development through systemic corruption to their advantage by employing:

- a series of intimidating practices against competitors;
- gentlemen's agreements whereby someone agreed to renounce to a job now to secure another (better) job later;
- agreements to exclude tenderers;
- bribery of managers to produce documentation or not to produce documentation required to progress a bid;
- forgery of public documents;
- collusion of private entrepreneurs, through private agreements, promises and coercion.

Research notes and emerging themes

The following themes have emerged from research fieldwork and notes as deserving of further attention and scrutiny, in no particular order:

A. The predominance of **antimafia investigations** over 'normal' investigations invests also the Port of Genova. There is a clear interest of the authority to identify potential interests for mafia groups operating in the area and the economy of the port. More research is needed to identify how mafia-type groups have evolved in their interests over the port of Genova.

B. Especially with reference to the **Calabrian mafia clans**, the 'ndrangheta, who are very well settled in the Liguria region, investigators pointed out the fact that large drug importations are organised by 'ndrangheta clans from Calabria rather than local ones. There seems to be a disconnection - or perhaps a disjuncture in capacity - between Calabrian-based 'ndrangheta clans engaged in drugs through the port of Genova, and Ligurian-based 'ndrangheta clans engaging in other activities on the territory.

C. Connected to the point above, the prominence of some groups or clans in activities in other ports (e.g. the Calabrian port of Gioia Tauro) provides individuals with knowledge of the port economy. This knowledge might be helpful in accessing other ports as well, as it represents a **specialist know-how** of the port system that is difficult to acquire for newcomers into this economy.

D. Most of the trafficking vicissitudes in Genova seem to be connected to **other ports of the Italian West coast**, such as Livorno or Napoli or Gioia Tauro. This connection across ports needs further scrutiny as it also relates to some of the main investors and companies active in these ports (i.e. MSC, Spinelli Group etc.).

E. The increasing attention of authorities to **waste trafficking** from Genova needs a standalone project of research that looks, at the very least, at: the legislative and regulatory frameworks of goods identifiable as 'waste'; the corporate and white-collar crime element of it; the routes and destination.

F. The port of Genova is tightly linked with its city and the economy of its region. This also seems to be true for what concerns organised crime manifestations. The port tends to mirror the city in terms of networks that operate both for drug distributions, engaging in infiltration into the economy and into corruption practices. An analysis of the **urban dimension of organised**

crime in Genova should complement any analysis of dimensions of organised crime in and around the port of Genova.
G. The elements emerging in relation to the port authority deserve more scrutiny, especially from a point of view of governance studies and anti-corruption studies. Discretionary powers, together with a criminal intent, might in fact affect **transparent governance** as much as hinder fair competition.

Case Study 2
Melbourne, Australia

Photo: Victorian Ports Melbourne Tower, March 2019, Author's rights

General information

The port of Melbourne is Australia's largest and busiest port[31], sitting at one end of the Yarra River on Port Phillip Bay and on 500 hectares of land bordering four municipalities in the state of Victoria. Over 3 million TEU[32] are handled annually at the port, with an average of 7200 containers and 1200 new motor vehicles per day crossing water and port land[33]. With a total trade value of over $100 billion, the port of Melbourne provides for a substantial portion of Victoria state economy. In March 2016, Victorian Parliament passed the *Delivering Victorian Infrastructure (Port of Melbourne Lease Transaction) Act 2016* (Vic). This legislation provided for the commercial operations of the port to be leased to the private sector for a period of 50 years and established **Victorian Ports Corporation (Melbourne)** as a the entity with responsibility for safe navigation and management of Station Pier as Victoria's cruise gateway and the **Port of Melbourne (PoM) Group** as the private leaseholder and strategic manager of the Port of Melbourne's commercial operations and assets.

More than **40 commercial shipping lines** call at the Port of Melbourne. The main routes to and from Melbourne port are

---

[31] https://www.portofmelbourne.com/about-us/

[32] Twenty-foot equivalent unit (TEU). A container size standard of twenty feet. Two twenty-foot containers (TEUs) equal one forty-foot equivalent unit (FEU). Container capacity and port capacity are frequently referred to in TEUs.

[33] https://www.portofmelbourne.com/about-us/quick-facts/

from New Zealand, Thailand, Malaysia, Japan, Taiwan, Indonesia, China, USA, and Germany.

With 21 km of waterfront, for 30 commercial berths, Melbourne port has 13 terminals, named and divided as piers, docks and wharfs: Swanson Dock, Appleton Dock, Webb Dock, Holden Dock, Gillibrand Pier, and South Wharf. There are three container terminals. ICTSI Group manages **VICT** (Victoria International Container Terminal), a fully automated terminal in Webb Dock 4 and 5. The other two container terminals are one in front of the other: East Swanson Dock terminal, with red cranes over four berths, is managed by **Patrick Containers**; West Swanson Dock terminal, with blue cranes also over four berths, is managed by **DP World Australia.** Both DP World Australia and Patrick Terminals have terminals also in Sydney, Brisbane and Fremantle (Perth) as well, dominating Australian port economy. DP World also manages Appleton Dock berths B, C and D for general cargo. Railway goods sidings serve both Swanson Dock East and West, so that containers can be moved between sea and rail transport. In order to increase terminal capacity and by-pass inner Melbourne roads, the Port Rail Transformation Project is on-going. This project (to be completed in 2023) includes restructuring the port rail land and asset commercial arrangements for leaseholders within the Swanson Dock East Precinct; new on-dock rail terminal capacity – development of a new on-dock rail terminal at Swanson Dock East; improved rail terminal operation arrangements and transparency between Port of Melbourne and Rail Terminal Operators.

Policing and Security Authorities

During the course of the research project, a total of 11 meetings were held, in the form of collective interviews, focus groups and/or individual interviews with: Victoria Police – Trident Task Force (Melbourne); Australian Federal Police – Organised Crime Command (Melbourne); Australian Border Force (Melbourne and Canberra); National Crime Agency (UK) Liaison Officer in Canberra; Home Affairs Department; Australian Criminal Intelligence Commission; Port of Melbourne Security; DP World and Patrick PFSOs (during tour of premises); Australian Commission for Law Enforcement Integrity.

Illicit Trafficking

Drug trafficking

According to the latest Illicit Drug Data Report[34] by the Australian Criminal Intelligence Commission, ATS (Amphetamine-type stimulants) accounted for the greatest proportion of the weight of border detections in 2017–18 by sea cargo, in line with trends across the nation as well. **Sea cargo is the importation stream accounting for the greatest proportion of the weight detected** for ATS for 2018 (64%) even though

---

[34] https://www.acic.gov.au/sites/default/files/illicit_drug_data_report_2017-18.pdf?v=1564727746

international mail remains the preferred stream for importation irrespective of weight. Also, sea cargo features prominently as importation stream accounting for the greatest proportion of the weight detected for cocaine (10.6%, even though air cargo reaches 76% instead), and it does not feature significantly for heroin and cannabis, while remaining low for MDMA, at 6%. It is expected, therefore, that in Melbourne, as in the rest of the country, when drugs arrive by container, they are more likely to be ATS, or cocaine, and to a lower extent also MDMA. In June 2019, 1.6 tons of meth, ice, for a total weight of, together with 37 kgs of heroin were found in vacuum-sealed bags inside stereo speakers. The drugs, coming from Bangkok, count so far for the largest seizure of meth in Australia, confirming the 'ice-crisis' that Australia has been facing for years[35].

One of the most famous operations of the past two decades, **Operation INCA**, from the AFP Melbourne, has taught some lessons about the role of the port in international drug trafficking. In August 2008, 4.4 tons of ecstasy (MDMA) - hidden in tomato tins - with a street value of $440 million were found in containers harbouring the port of Melbourne, and originating from Italy, and led to the arrest of 20 people across Australia. Behind the shipment was a network based in Melbourne, with contacts in South Australia and New South Wales, affiliated to Calabrian mafia clans in Australia and in communication with

---

[35] Parliamentary Joint Committee On Law Enforcement - Inquiry into Crystal Methamphetamine (Ice) - Victoria Police Submission July 2015

their Calabrian partners. In the charging and conviction of **Rob Karam**[36] the court depicted his role in this network, as one of the wholesale consumers:

i. To initially provide an identity to be associated with a declared consignment that would safely provide the cover for the concealed cocaine.
ii. To provide relevant consignment and fake information so at to facilitate early identification of the arriving container.
iii. To provide updated information regarding whether the container would be able to be safely accessed offside.
iv. To liaise with a third party so as to achieve that safe access to the contraband, its removal and its ultimate delivery to interested parties.
v. To provide the confirmation as to what was going to happen in the days after the arrival of the container.

Crucially, Mr. Karam reported to **Pasquale Barbaro**[37] (the responsible person for, and the financier of, the job) that there were problems with the container, in that it was being watched by authorities and that it was too dangerous to proceed with any attempt to access the container.

The shipping container was addressed to a **legitimate business** 'Trans Global Food Brokers'. However, the designated business/consignee had no knowledge of the shipment, and no

---

[36] DPP vs Rob Karam, [2015] VCC 855; R v Karam (Unreported Supreme Court of Victoria, King J, 24 May 2012 (date of conviction), 30 April 2013 (date of sentence)); Karam v R, [2015] VSCA 50
[37] DPP v Barbaro, [2009] VSC 27

involvement in having arranged it. The plan was that the container and its contents would be diverted to a person whose contact details had been provided separately. When safe, the container would be removed, and taken elsewhere to be unloaded, stored, and its contents ultimately distributed.

The same network had also been responsible, in July 2008, for the arrival of 150 kgs of cocaine, hidden in coffee beans from Colombia. Another shipment, containing about 100 kg of pseudoephedrine from India was also expected but was later discovered to be a scam to buyers. In these cases, as well, Mr. Karam provided **strategic advice** as to **shipping documentation** and as to which port the container should be offloaded.

Since the arrests linked to these shipments, scenarios of drug importations and trafficking to Melbourne has obviously evolved, but still retaining the **following recurring characteristics** already visible since Operation Inca:
1. The criminal networks remain highly multi-ethnic;
2. The origin countries are commodity-specific (from European transit for cocaine; Asian transit and origin for heroin and ATS).
3. City brokers handle various drugs through various routes.

In an **operation of October 2013**, one of the largest multi-agency operations involving joint waterfront taskforces in Brisbane (Jericho), Sydney (Polaris) and Melbourne (Trident), as well as the Sydney-based Joint Organised Crime Group and the Melbourne-based Joint Organised Crime Taskforce, led to the arrest of three people and the seizure of more than 200kg of methamphetamine concealed in tyres of a Sinotruk Hova terminal tractor truck on a ship arriving from China (Shanghai) via Japan. Two of the three men arrested were dock workers in Victoria. The truck had been imported by Motek Engineering Pty Ltd, a company owned by Patrick Cini, who was then charged and convicted for importation of a border-controlled drug. The truck, headed to Melbourne, was actually stopped in Brisbane port, the drugs confiscated and substituted with an inert crystalline substance to activate a law enforcement-**controlled delivery**. When the truck docked at Patrick Terminal, in Melbourne, Cini and his associates went to collect it to move it to the Motek's factory. The case unfolded from there to build the criminal case[38]. The case does not contain more details on the network on the other side, in China.

Operation Afloat, in June 2017, led to the arrest of seven men in Melbourne who were trying to import around 92 kgs of cocaine in three black duffle bags hidden in a cargo container from Panama[39]. Trident Taskforce, at the time composed of AUSTRAC (Australian Transaction Reports and Analysis Centre), AFP, ABF, ACIC, the Australian Taxation Office and of course Victoria Police, was formed in 2013 as Commonwealth-funded

---

[38] R v Cini [2014] VSC 409 (29 August 2014)
[39] https://newsroom.abf.gov.au/releases/international-drug-syndicate-disrupted-by-seven-arrests-in-melbourne

maritime taskforce aimed at detecting and disrupting organised crime at the state's waterfront[40].

The network in question had also run various shipments for months, observed by investigators. They also had a **mentor** in a **businessman** in **Melbourne** who helped different people in the criminal network to buy properties and assets, reinvest their proceeds of crime in shares and companies' names and advice on drug trade as well.

Among those arrested were Canadian, Australian and British men, as the network relied mostly on **Canadian and Vietnamese connections** in Colombia. The Australia/Canada/Vietnam connection is not new to Australia, as courts have heard in different cases[41] in the past ten years and not only in Melbourne. For example, in a case in 2012[42], a shipment of foot spas and pedicure chairs arrived in Melbourne from Canada concealing cocaine, methamphetamine and MDMA. One of the defendants, **Tang**, a Canadian citizen, was present when the drugs departed Canada as his role was to confirm the same quantity arrived in Australia. Other defendant **Pham**, also Vietnamese-Canadian, acted as a point of liaison between the importers of the drugs and the freight forwarding company (by paying their fees),

---

[40] Originally, waterfront taskforces were set up in Brisbane (Jericho), Sydney (Polaris) and Melbourne (Trident) but as of today only Trident still exists, with funding extended in 2016 (but without the AFP) -
https://newsroom.abf.gov.au/releases/trident-task-force-funding-extended
[41] DPP (Cth) v Brown [2017] VSCA 162 (23 June 2017); McCraw v The Queen [2011] NSWCCA 162;
[42] Pham v The Queen; Tang v The Queen [2012] VSCA 101

facilitating delivery of the container to the warehouse and unpacking the contents to deliver them to the purchaser. Both played a material role in the movement of drugs from Melbourne after their arrival into Australia. Pham was also involved in another case in NSW in 2020[43], also for the importation of foot spas secreting cocaine and methamphetamine from Canada, together with her cousin **Nguyen**. Nguyen had set up a business, registered two business names and leased a commercial warehouse in Victoria, but also rented a storage space in Sydney. He was present to take delivery, deconstructed the foot spas to remove the packages of drugs and attended with Pham to hand over the packages to the purchaser. Nguyen was born in Vietnam but had migrated to Australia in 1982.

What else can be learned from cases of drug importations into Melbourne?

1. **Technology** has progressively helped cross-pollination of different ethnic groups, it helped **"de-ethnicise"** organised crime groups and activities.
2. There is an **'island effect'** for proceeds of crime. Money tends to be reinvested in Melbourne or in Australia, as this might be easier than sending the money to launder somewhere else outside the country. Usually these processes are facilitated by **professional brokers** in the

---

[43] R v Nguyen; R v Pham [2010] NSWCCA 238; (2010) 205 A Crim R 106

city, who also support the criminal network in procuring other transport services, or infrastructure (i.e. mobile phones, cars, bank accounts).
3. The **variety of shipment methods**, from printers to foot spas, from coffee beans to stereo speakers, is a sign of the variety of routes. Illicit drugs are not necessarily arriving in Melbourne ports, but can be moved to Melbourne from other ports, and from Melbourne ports also go to other locations. Beyond sea shipments, air and mail cargos are actually confirmed as more frequent ways to import drugs in the country.
4. Networks usually copy companies' names and addresses to import as legitimate suppliers. They **exploit the reputation of companies** with good names to avoid extra checks.
5. Even though containers remain a preferred method of shipment, **other vessels**, also including personal yacht are also frequent. Frequent can also be smaller vessels (concealing the drugs inside the vessels or in its structure or even underneath) that approach the container ships in water or nearby the port.
6. **Corruption** of government officials paid off **in foreign jurisdictions** in cocaine or money to allow things to go through their port has been observed.
7. **Corruption in Australia**, of government officials, or dock workers are also observed consistently, notwithstanding the changes to recruitment strategies for dock workers

and the calls for transparency in the recruitment of border and government officials.
8. The authorities have started paying Increased attention to ownership and management of **warehouses** around the port area, as these play a crucial role when handling containers and cargo in and out of the city.

Counterfeit and illicit tobacco trade

According to a report on Illicit Tobacco in Australia, drafted by KPMG in 2018[44], whilst the volume of overall tobacco consumption declined, the proportion of illicit tobacco consumption increased from 14.3% to 15.0% in 2017/2018. In particular, contraband consumption accounted for the majority of total illicit tobacco consumption, increasing to 51.1% of the total illicit consumption (or 1.20 million kg) in 2017 from 38.5% in 2016. Flows of Chinese and Indonesian labelled packs were the largest non-domestic inflows accounting for 25% and 6% of the total non-domestic flows in 2017 respectively. In the meanwhile, unbranded (or 'Chop Chop') consumption accounts for 47% of total illicit consumption even though the volume of unbranded tobacco decreased overall.

During fieldwork for this project, it became quote clear that illicit tobacco represents a real challenge for border forces

---

[44] KPMG LLP, Strategy Group, 2018, Illicit Tobacco in Australia, Full Year Report 2017, London

in Australia. Illicit tobacco is either grown or produced locally or procured illegally from overseas markets without the payment of customs duties. In particular, we can divide illicit tobacco into **manufactured** cigarettes, which could be **counterfeit, contraband or illicit whites**[45], or **unbranded** tobacco, which includes **chop-chop or pre-filled tubes**[46]. Interestingly, tobacco can only be grown in Australia (for personal or commercial use) with an excise license but there are no current licenses for tobacco growing in Australia and therefore no tobacco is legally grown in Australia for any purpose. The illicit tobacco trade deprives the community of taxes and therefore is for Australian Border Force to curb. In July 2018, **the Illicit Tobacco Taskforce (ITTF)** was established to protect Commonwealth revenue by *"proactively targeting, disrupting and dismantling serious actors and organised crime syndicates that deal in illicit tobacco"*[47]. This ABF-led taskforce brings together the expertise of ABF and Department of Home Affairs, the Australian Criminal Intelligence Commission (ACIC), the Australian Transaction Reports and Analysis Centre (AUSTRAC), the Commonwealth Director of

---

[45] Illicit Whites are manufactured cigarettes that are usually manufactured legally in one country/market but which the evidence suggests have been smuggled across borders during their transit to Australia, where they have limited or no legal distribution and are sold without the payment of tax.
[46] Unbranded tobacco is usually sold as finely cut loose leaf tobacco in 250g or half kilogram amounts. It carries no labelling or health warnings and is sold in pre-filled tubes or loose in bags (called Chop Chop).
[47] https://www.abf.gov.au/about-us/taskforces/illicit-tobacco-taskforce

Public Prosecutions (CDPP) and the Australian Taxation Office (ATO).

The mechanisms of shipment for illicit tobacco are similar to those for shipments of drugs as we can summarise the challenges of this trade to Australian borders as follows:

i. The risks are low, and the profits are high, which means the **volume** of this trade is **higher** than drugs.
ii. There is a wide understanding that the illegal tobacco trade serves as **funding** for other organised crime activities, especially as it provides cash flow. However, there are groups that solely deal in illicit tobacco for cash accumulation, with financiers that might also be businessmen in the city or based elsewhere.
iii. There is, however, also a **cultural element** to illicit trade of tobacco. In fact, ABF agents link the consumption of illegal tobacco to ethnic and cultural heritage, whereby different ethnic groups tend to use, or are more willing to use, tobacco from their own places of origin at lower costs.
iv. The illegal tobacco market is deeply interwoven with the legal tobacco trade, which is heavily taxed. The legal retailers use the **same points of sale** in Melbourne for both legal and illegal tobacco sales.
v. Illicit trade of tobacco has, as most common **origin countries**, Malaysia, Taiwan, China and India, with South-European, Middle Asian and Chinese networks heavily involved in the business.

As said, these trades are **frequent and high in volume and weight**. In December 2019, on Boxing Day, the Australian Border Force seized about one million illicit cigarettes from an air cargo shipment as it arrived into Sydney. The day after the ITTF was alerted by an overseas partner agency to a shipment arriving into Melbourne that they suspected to be undeclared cigarettes. The ABF examined the container and discovered 9.8 million cigarettes fraudulently declared as 'dough mixers', 'cake fridges' and 'freezers' and the estimated duty evasion was nearly $9 million. A third large sea cargo shipment arrived into Melbourne from Hong Kong in early January 2020 and was found to contain more than 1.5 tons of rough-cut tobacco concealed within table tops. This detection was as a result of information passed on from authorities in Hong Kong and the shipment had an estimated evaded duty value of $1.9 million[48]. This followed another large seizure in Melbourne in early December 2019, when the Australian Border Force (ABF) detected and seized over 39 million illicit cigarettes in one week[49].

Furthermore, as said, the risks of smuggling tobacco are considered generally much lower than smuggling drugs. In, abovementioned **Operation Inca**, two of the defendants, Jon Visser and Carmelo Falanga[50], claimed, as part of their defence,

---

[48] https://newsroom.abf.gov.au/releases/international-cooperation-assists-in-the-seizure-of-smuggled-tobacco
[49] https://newsroom.abf.gov.au/releases/over-39-million-illicit-cigarettes-seized-in-melbourne
[50] Visser v The Queen; Falanga v The Queen [2015] VSCA 168 (26 June 2015)

that they *believed* that the container held a large quantity of illicit tobacco ('chop-chop') and not drugs. Also, a defence witness for Visser claimed that, during a conversation between two of the organisers of the drug shipment, Barbaro and Zirilli, the following was said – which also shows the perception that **tobacco remains safer than drugs, as illicit trade**.

Zirilli: We should have stayed doing tobacco containers as this here is a disaster.

Barbaro: Bit late for that now.

Zirilli: When we were getting sentenced did you hear that they might be charging Johnny Visser?

Barbaro: I can't understand why? We told Johnny that the container was full of tobacco and I never mentioned eccies to him.

Zirilli: Yeah I remember you saying to Johnny that there was $4 to $5 million worth of tobacco in the container and we never mentioned eccies to him.

Another case that shows the **autonomy** and the **endurance** of some criminal networks smuggling illicit tobacco through the port of Melbourne, was the case against businessman **Nabil Grege** and his associates in 2013[51]. The case was about the importation of two containers into Melbourne that contained illicit whites. Nabil Grege run a property development business called The First Stone in Northcote,

---

[51] DPP v Nabil Grege and James Grege, Prosecution Opening Statement, 21 February 2018

Melbourne, together with other international businesses too, such as a logging enterprise in Cameroon. On one side the network needed to secure a smooth shipment from the Emirates (with the cigarettes originating in Lebanon): the Custom broker for the containers he and his son had arranged to ship to Melbourne containing the illicit tobacco, was a company named Stokes and Bells; Patlin Transport was the trucking company who was supposed to help with the movement of the containers from Patrick Terminals. On the other side, it was necessary to gather information about the status of the containers, to find out when and whether it was safe to collect them. The contact here was Dean Crimes, a person who worked for Toll Shipping, who declared he was waiting for information from an employee of Patrick Terminal. While the shipment went wrong for the network for a mixture of law enforcement surveillance and substitutions of containers and goods, this case before court showed the intricated organised nature that illicit tobacco trade can take.

Other illicit trade

In terms of **inward** trafficking, Australia and Melbourne don't differ much from other countries and ports. Beyond drugs and tobacco, other goods are obviously smuggled into the country, from wildlife to pharmaceuticals, although these have not featured much in the findings of this project. Of interest remained investigations into goods that are imported into

Victoria, avoiding the payment of Duty and the Goods and Services Tax[52].

Outward trafficking has also not featured much, even though, in conversation, investigators have pointed out that there is **no real control** over containers that leave the country, and that things like containers full of cash as much, in different currencies, as containers full of undeclared goods have been accidentally found by ABF in the course of other controls or random checks that are at times carried out. The emphasis has historically always been on importation. There are, however, global obligations for exports, such as nuclear materials or arms technology, in which case there is an **export control authority**, a department within the Ministry of **Defence**. In these cases, ABF would work with this authority, but only upon specific needs.

Waste trafficking from Australia has been flagged as an emerging issue. In May 2019[53], the news reported that Holcim Philippines Inc. had officially imported materials to the Philippines from Australia, at Mindanao International Container Terminal, allegedly for use in its plants. In Manila, an inspection was made and showed that it contained shredded municipal wastes such as scrap plastic, cellophane, wrappers, textile, stones, and soil among others. The issue provoked a small diplomatic incident and it adds to the complaints of countries such as Indonesia and the Philippines, who claim they have

---

[52] https://newsroom.abf.gov.au/releases/import-duty-evader-to-pay-2-million
[53] https://cnnphilippines.com/news/2019/5/23/denr-emb-customs-fuel-holcim-australia-mismis-oriental.html

become the dumping sites of richer countries, such as Australia[54]. This type of criminality, as in the case of Genova, reflects corporate liabilities and white-collar crimes in dealing with **recycling and waste disposal**. They eventually are organised crime in the sense that they can be harmful as much as they can be profitable. Indeed, according to a report for the Department of the Environment in 2017[55], in Australia, the recycling and resource recovery industry is undermined by bad landfill levy design at the state level. The report concludes[56] that *"levy alignment led by the Commonwealth would stop perverse outcomes such as interstate waste trafficking. In addition, waste levy revenue should be confined to waste management and resource recovery initiatives and illegal dumping, not propping up state budgets".*

---

[54]https://www.scmp.com/news/asia/southeast-asia/article/3027973/indonesia-sending-back-547-containers-hazardous-waste;https://www.smh.com.au/world/asia/indonesia-rejects-toxic-australian-plastic-recycling-20190701-p5235f.html

[55] Blue Environment and Randall Environmental Consulting, 2017, Australian National Waste Report 2016, Prepared for the Department of the Environment and Energy
https://www.environment.gov.au/system/files/resources/d075c9bc-45b3-4ac0-a8f2-6494c7d1fa0d/files/national-waste-report-2016.pdf

[56] Ibid., page 28

Infiltration in the legal economy, corruption and governance issues

Beyond illicit trades, organised and complex crime at port of Melbourne manifests through different forms of corruption, as an enabler and as an autonomous practice to infiltrate the port economy as much as to affect port governance and development.

There are four main issues that can be brought forward when it comes to **corruption and illicit governance in the port of Melbourne**, ranging from occasional to systemic forms of corruption, collusion and malpractices:

> 1. The issuing of **MSICs (Maritime Security Identification Cards)**, the problems of access to terminals and the allegations/perceptions of systemic corruption in the port workforce.

Conversations with port of Melbourne managers, including PFSOs of the two main terminals DP World and Patrick, emphasised problems with the MSIC scheme. MSIC are identification cards that were introduced in 2007 to conform the seaports to the airports and their Aviation Security Identification Card. MSIC certify that the holder has met the minimum security requirements to work unescorted or unmonitored in a maritime security zone; they are not intended as access cards as ports or port facilities still can control access to their own zones. The background check is obviously done against certain serious offences (i.e. terrorism, treason, use of weapons of mass destruction; hijacking of a plane or a ship) and other criminal record checks done by the AFP and ASIO (Australian Security Intelligence Organisation). MSIC are perceived as a risk in the port facility's business. While for some participants definitely *"MSIC provide a pathway to criminality"*, the debate on their actual ability to curb criminality on the waterfront is ongoing[57]. The problems with MSIC are linked to the following considerations:

   a. MSIC provide access to the port precinct, but they get lost, they don't get updated that often (2 or 4 years of validity), they don't always get returned when expired (as it is requested instead), and the port sector has a high turnover of staff. Some MSIC holders can offer their services to others for hire, temporarily. Provided that someone in a truck has a MSIC (driver or client) the truck can access port zones. MSIC are not necessarily smart card; they don't come with an in-built chip, which makes the difference between being an ID card (no functioning expiry) or an access card (with functioning expiry).
   b. They can be obtained without a photographic proof of identity (thus using other people's names and documents, i.e. birth certificate).

---

[57] Joint Committee on the Australian Crime Commission Reference:
Adequacy of aviation and maritime security measures to combat serious and organised crime Thursday, 18 February 2010 Sydney

c. The Department of Infrastructure, Transport, Regional Development and Local Government authorises organisations to serve as an approved MSIC Issuing Body. There are currently 15 authorised MSIC Issuing Bodies[58]. Most of the container terminal staff are issued through 1-Stop, which is a national organisation set up by DP World and Patrick (used also as booking system to enter the facilities), while other issuers, such as Sydney Ports Corporations can issue MSIC to other services working around the port, and are also the issuing body for Port of Melbourne.
d. The disqualifying offences for a MSIC (over 100 and soon in 2020 over 200) are mostly related to terrorism and other personal or infrastructure-related security threat. Transnational organised crime, people smuggling, drug importation and money laundering were added to the list later on and do not automatically preclude the issuing of a MSIC.
e. Port authorities and terminals are not law enforcement agencies and therefore their priority remains trade; individual security companies which are contracted by terminals operate security checks of MSIC.

The **Costigan Commission** (officially named the Royal Commission on the Activities of the Federated Ship Painters and

---

[58] https://www.homeaffairs.gov.au/about-us/our-portfolios/transport-security/identity/issuing-bodies/msic

Dockers Union) was an Australian Royal Commission in the 1980s, set up to investigate criminal activities, including violence and organised crime, associated with the Painters and Dockers Union, with special reference to Melbourne port and waterfront. Leading to the set-up of the National Crime Authority in 1984, the Costigan Commission four volumes report on many members of the union that were involved in a wide range of criminal activities and also led to profound changes in the union itself. The reputation of *wharfies* (port workers) and of the maritime union (currently MUA, Maritime Union of Australia) as corrupt and generationally still linked to organised crime figures in the city remains almost intact. As noticed by investigators:

"Organised crime is still embedded in the port, through families and friends of dockworkers; they still manipulate things [including MSIC cards and access]. Corruption in the family environment of dockworkers has never been really targeted or taken away; they still control the port, who they work with, what shifts they work, with what cruise they work with...the large numbers of companies can't do anything about it; the crooks know the system way better than the businessmen do"

In February 2020, Trident Task Force charged two men for alleged drug trafficking at a port facility in Melbourne[59]. The two **port (dock) workers** were allegedly dealing drugs directly from the company they were working for in Port of Melbourne. The case is before the courts but tends to confirm how the port environment in Melbourne remains vulnerable to criminal activities and exploitation of territory and industry-specific specialism.

> 2. **Border corruption**, and allegations/expectations of connivance in criminal activities of border agents and government officials.

Together with port workers, the issue of corruption-enabled organised crime in the port of Melbourne relates heavily to involvement of border agents and other government officials in bribery and corruption schemes. To address the risk of border officials using their positions to assist criminal networks, a joint AFP/ Australian Commission for Law Enforcement Integrity (ACLEI) Taskforce was established in 2011 in New South Wales, but not in Victoria, and mainly for the aviation environment and to a lesser extent the maritime sector in NSW (e.g. Operations

---

[59] https://www.miragenews.com/two-men-charged-as-part-of-port-investigation/ and https://www.police.vic.gov.au/two-men-charged-part-port-investigation

Heritage[60], Bagatelle, Minium[61]). Operation Heritage (2014) in particular has had a lasting effect on both Customs, its successor the ABF, as well as on ACLEI itself. It is reported that Heritage *"resulted in considerable changes to Custom's integrity policy, practice and organisational arrangements"*[62].

Most of the cases collected or indicated by participants in this research revolved around Sydney and the aviation sector, with evidence of individual bribes and also more systemic forms of corruption whereby custom agents were working together with, and for, the Australian criminal group of the Bra Boys, characterised for their surfer culture. Alleged connections between the group, border force, security officers were also suspected at Sydney port.

The absence of evidence is not evidence of absence, in this case, and it is the opinion of most of the participants, that for Melbourne we are indeed in a case of **evidence of absence** for lack of scrutiny, rather than for lack of the phenomenon. The media reported about three confidential national anti-corruption operations, two of which codenamed Operation Arrowhead and Operation Dureau in early 2010s, which

---

[60] https://www.aclei.gov.au/sites/default/files/report022013-operationheritageinterimreport.pdf?v=1455097900

[61] Australian Federal Police (2015) Parliamentary Joint Committee on the Australian Commission for Law Enforcement Integrity Inquiry into the integrity of Australia's border arrangements

[62] https://www.aph.gov.au/Parliamentary_Business/Committees/Joint/Australian_Commission_for_Law_Enforcement_Integrity/Jurisdiction_of_ACLEI/Report/c02

identified suspected threats to Australia's border security in both Sydney and Melbourne, in the form of connivance of custom officers (the ABF's current restructuring happened in 2015) with middle-Eastern, Balkan, Italian and Australian crime groups, mostly for drug importations[63]. In fact, ACLEI made a number of comments to the 2015 Inquiry into the integrity of Australia's border arranged, that can be summarised as follows[64] and could be considered a good summary of the red flags identified in Melbourne too:

- evidence of private illicit drug use by public officials, which brings them into potential compromise by organised crime groups;
- the risk posed by 'back office' staff who may have access to sensitive law enforcement information, but who often are subject to lesser scrutiny than front-line officers
- vulnerabilities in specific border operating environments, such as airport and quarantine clearance environments, and
- the prospect of 'vertical collusion', whereby Federal and State officials might collude in corruption enabled border crime.

---

[63] https://www.smh.com.au/national/outgunned-federal-corruption-agencies-not-up-to-the-task-20181125-p50i6i.html

[64] Parliamentary Joint Committee on the Australian Commission for Law Enforcement Integrity Inquiry into the integrity of Australia's border arrangements Submission by the Australian Commission for Law Enforcement Integrity 2015

In January 2019, the media[65] reported on Victoria Police charging two **Department of Agriculture & Water Resource employees** for doing unauthorised container checks to assess their custom status and whether there was any Border Force flags on them. These individuals were both linked to organised crime groups in Melbourne, and in particular to Middle-Eastern groups. The case is currently before the court, which heard evidence in relation to charges of bribery and dishonesty related to the defendants' roles overseeing the inspection of items, including shipping containers, through customs. The overall operation was linked to the importation of illegal cigarettes. One of the defendants was acting assistant director at the Department of Agricutlure and Water Resources and, due to its relationship with a prominent organised crime individual, was under threat. This individual was also believed to have taken a bribe from an undercover officer.

3. The system of **trusted insiders** and corruption in the supply chain and services provisions.

As the Australian Border Force is a law enforcement agency part of the Department of **Home Affairs**, it is Home Affairs that runs the intelligence and the risk profiles upon which

---

[65] Simonis, Anika, Official in crime gang link - Government boss accused of bribery, dishonesty, in Herald Sun Melbourne, 17 January 2019

ABF then acts. Looking at **supply chain service providers** (customers' broker, freight forwarders, licensed deposits etc) and how they facilitate or collude with organised crime is one of the main focus of this intelligence work. Australian Taxation Office (ATO) would be investigating cartels of corporations within their financial crime taskforces. The search for **trusted insiders' threats** - employee or recurring client in a position to exploit a security system to conduct or enable an act of unlawful interference - remains challenging. But promoting similar standards of trade, through a **trusted trader scheme**, remains fundamental for both Home Affairs and the terminals.

Operation Boscobel in 2015 led to the arrest of six men by Trident Taskforce for charges of conspiracy to dishonestly cause a loss to the Commonwealth, fraud and evidence of money laundering and links to organised crime groups, especially for possession of firearms[66]. The charges were brought forward by ATO and involved ACG Security, one of Australia's biggest private security services. ACG was acquired by Spotless, retaining Port of Melbourne, including Patrick Stevedoring, among other clients. Just after the news broke about the acquisition, police froze the $10 million paid for the

---

[66] https://www.heraldsun.com.au/news/law-order/six-charged-over-alleged-8-million-tax-fraud/news-story/fe6b3ef42fd5d1ef47775f378ca44040

takeover due to pending investigation on ACG and pending licence suspension too[67].

Things to note about this case:
  i. The charges related to a loss to the Australian Tax Office ('ATO') of Pay As You Go ('PAYG') tax neither withheld, declared nor remitted to the ATO. Supplemental untaxed cash payments were regularly paid to ten salaried employees of the company.
  ii. ACG made use of a number of sub-contractors, some of which also linked to ACG personnel involved in Operation Boscobel.
  iii. Even though ACG projected an image eschewing any reliance upon sub-contractors, a large number of guards were actually employees of several sub-contractors to ACG. ACG asserted overarching control in the recruitment, deployment and supervision of guard personnel, whether they were employed directly by ACG or through its several sub-contractors.
  iv. ACG was obliged to withhold an amount of PAYG tax from wages and salaries paid to its employees and to regularly remit that amount to the ATO. That responsibility shifted from ACG to retained

---

[67] https://www.heraldsun.com.au/news/law-order/police-suspend-acg-securitys-licence/news-story/2aaf80ab82b71b5c153f70cd6d11025f

> sub-contractors in respect of their employees' wages.
>
> v. Korras, Ammouchi and Moussa[68] persistently acted dishonestly by paying 'off the books' wages to security guard employees without remitting PAYG tax to the ATO.

Aside from the loss to the Commonwealth and the charges by ATO, this operation exposed the risks of insider threats by trusted companies and insiders to the Port of Melbourne. The risks were:

- **Abuse of trust** of trusted insider relationship with the client, Port of Melbourne and the terminals, landlords of the port. Abuse of entrusted power for private gain.
- Through the **delegation** to sub-contractors, **lack of oversight over recruitment** and also over who had **access to information**, files and insider data (i.e. the security plans, ships' info etc) that were shared with ACG but eventually also accessible to sub-contractors as delegated powers.
- As some intelligence in Boscobel also pointed out, some of the guards recruited by sub-contractors were suspected to **facilitate organised crime activities**, and specifically firearm and drug trafficking. Also, accounting

---

[68] R v Moussa [2019] VCC 1891 (25 October 2019); DPP v Korras [2019] VCC 1681 (8 October 2019)

firms and lawyers and other professional facilitators supporting ACG also were suspected to have links with organised crime figures.
- Infiltration of the security services could prove crucial for access, entry and exit and **knowledge of the overall security protocols** and systems in order to elude them.

    4. Corruption and collusion in contracts relating to **construction, development and infrastructures**.

When the Independent Board of Anti-corruption Commission (IBAC) for Victoria was given new investigative powers in 2015[69], a question was raised on whether these powers could have applied also to political corruption. While this was still subject to interpretation of the new regulations, stalling on the legislation for the port leases was stalled for risks of IBAC interference[70]. This project has not found direct and open evidence of corruption and illicit governance of markets and industries of construction, infrastructure and the overall development of the port of Melbourne.

It is again a matter of evidence of absence, as most of the cases discussed in this project that relate to high level corruption don't relate to Victoria, but to New South Wales.

---

[69] https://www.ibac.vic.gov.au/investigating-corruption/our-investigative-powers

[70] https://www.afr.com/companies/infrastructure/corruption-threat-stalls-melbourne-port-sale-20160128-gmg4xx

In 2016, **Operation Spicer**, by the Independent Commission Against Corruption (ICAC) for NSW, made a recommendation to prosecutors to proceed against Joseph Tripodi for the offence of misconduct in public office. Misusing his position as a member of Parliament for Labour, Mr Tripodi had provided of a confidential Treasury report to representatives of the private corporation Buildev Group Pty Ltd, without lawful authority to do so, in exchange for future benefits. This followed Minister of Roads, Maritime and Freight for New South Wales, Duncan Gay, confirming the existence of a very confidential agreement of "cross payments" to compensate the owners of rival ports Botany and Kembla, if Newcastle's container volumes pass an agreed limit[71] (of about $100 per container unit (about $1 million per vessel) it handled above a threshold of 30,000 a year). Current investigations (**Operation Ember**[72]) by ICAC in NSW also invest Roads and Maritime Services (RMS) employees and how they exercised their official functions when awarding consulting and construction contracts in NSW ports.

Such cases are examples of high-end corruption and complex crimes also for Victoria. As noticed by officers in Trident Taskforce:

---

[71] Legislative Council Parliamentary Debates (Hansard) Fifty-Sixth Parliament First Session, Tuesday, 13 September 2016

[72] https://www.icac.nsw.gov.au/investigations/current-investigations/2019/operation-ember

"To say that these cases don't happen here...I wouldn't go that far. [...] When construction contracts in or around the ports are involved, big roads or new cranes for example, various agencies have responsibility to check integrity...it can't be said that there isn't unduly influence for sure... there is no reason why something like that couldn't happen here – there are lots of powerful people that have connections to the port".

Research notes and emerging themes

The following themes have emerged from research fieldwork and notes as deserving of further attention and scrutiny, in no particular order:

A. The port is that environment where **everyone knows what everyone else is doing**. It has been observed that it is specifically the case for stevedores, who know each other across Australia, as much as abroad as well, and this facilitates business, including illicit business.
B. The port environment is full of regulations and norms, but **informality reigns**. There are things that in theory authorities are told no one can do in a terminal, but then testing them at the port, authorities learn that they can indeed be done (i.e. moving containers to a certain place, checking or not checking certain locations, moving shifts and rotas etc).

C. Law enforcement agencies, in the maritime environment, look for **systems and processes**, but the whole environment is very disorganised, there is possibility for manipulation and confusion of systems and processes. Industry practices are not what expected by law enforcement.
D. There seems to be a decrease of the use of containers for drug importations; the system of using a **mother-daughter ship** (a smaller ships to which the cargo is partially offloaded to at sea). This could be a vessel or a personal **yacht:** these represent the most common ways to import drugs by sea without touching the ports.
E. Intelligence is about relationship and in Victoria this is an issue, as **occupational culture** of the different authorities, together with different security protocols across institutions, prevent a real sharing of intelligence across platforms.
F. A lot of what was discussed in Victoria does not come from Victorian examples, but is discussed as **evidence by absence**. Mainly it is about NSW and discussed by comparison and lesson learned. The importance of **Joint Task Force Polaris** in 2012 has affected the way maritime crime and waterfront criminality are seen across the whole of Australia.
G. There is an indication, or an intuition, of a **'waterfall effect'** – the level of sophistication of criminal activities of organised crime groups in the city falls onto the port. For example, even though there is an understanding that

most of drug importations are ethnically hybrid, the satellite industries – logistics and transports – might not be. Authorities indicate that Italian clans are heavily involved in the transport and logistics, as much as Chinese/Asian clans are involved instead in the laundering of money, which mirrors in the role and the social positions of these organised crime groups in the city to a certain extent.

H. There seems to be little understanding on how to approach instances of **corruption** in cases of **large infrastructure projects** affecting the maritime zone, i.e. the Melbourne Port Rail Shuttle[73]. The oversight of integrity and transparency seems to be spread across a number of authorities, not all of which law enforcement ones. As for the abovementioned waterfall effect, there are figures – mostly entrepreneur – who could exercise some unduly influence over contracts and procurements, as they are both well connected in the city's business field as much as they have links with some organised crime figures.

---

[73] The current Port Rail Shuttle plan, which is effectively the first major initiative proposed by the Lonsdale Group the new owners of the port of Melbourne, foresees the establishment of a Port Rail Shuttle (PRS) which will operate between a portside Metropolitan Intermodal Terminal (MIRT) and two suburban terminals, one in the north located at Somerton and one in the south west at Altona.

Case Study 3
Montreal, Canada

Photo: Termont Terminal July 2019, Author's rights

General information

The second largest port of Canada after Vancouver, and therefore the first on the Canadian East Coast, the port of Montreal stretches for 26 kilometres following the St Lawrence's river over the Ile of Montreal; since the boom of container shipping in the 1960s, the working port has in fact moved away from the city centre. Strategically located 1,000 miles inland and close to the consumer market of the US Midwest as much as Eastern Canada and the routes to Europe, the port of Montreal is a one-stop port with no intermediate calls to discharge and load ships. Direct services to and from Montreal comprise the Caribbeans and the US, Norther Europe, including Antwerp, Liverpool, Hmburg, Rotterdam and the Mediterranean routes, including Genova, Gioia Tauro, Valencia, Livorno. Transhipment ports of call comprise Latina America, including Santos, Montevideo, Buenos Aires, Cartagena, the Middle East (e.g. Istanbul, Abu Dhabi), Africa (e.g. Lagos, Mombasa) and Asia, including ports of China, Thailand, Japan and Australian/New Zealand ports. In terms of main routes for trade to Montreal, the most distinctive is the one from North Europe (37% of containers) followed by Asian ports (21%) with access to Panama and Suez Canals. The port has weekly exchanges with some of the major North European and Mediterranean ports such as: Antwerp, Rotterdam, Genoa, Liverpool, Gioia Tauro, Hamburg, Valencia[74].

---

[74] https://www.tradingwiththeworld.com/en/index.snc

There are ten terminals in Montreal, five of which are container terminals (Terminal Cast and Terminal Racine operated by Montreal Gateway Terminals Partnership -MGT, Maisonneve and Viau Terminals operated by Termont, Bickerdike Terminal operated by Empire Stevedoring). With a volume of trade of 1.4 million TEU per year, and with plans to expand containership in the farther territory of Contrecoeur are on the way, the port of Montreal serves Quebec and Ontario with a total of $41 billion in goods every year through over 2,000 vessels a week and 2,500 trucks per day[75]. The economic impact of the port of Montreal is huge, with over 16,000 direct, indirect and induced jobs and an estimated of $2.1 billion in added value for the Canadian economy[76].

The Montreal Port Authority operates the Port of Montreal. The port authority is an autonomous self-financing federal agency that builds and maintains infrastructures then leased to private stevedoring companies. Montreal is in fact a landlord port.

Policing and Security Authorities

Since 2004 - when the port became the first Canadian port to be accredited by the International Ship and Port Security (ISPS) Code- security at the port of Montreal is delivered through

---

[75] https://www.port-montreal.com/files/PDF/publications/2015-07-28_jaquette-corpo-en.pdf
[76] Port of Montreal, 2019, Directory.

an integrated plan. As each terminal, under Canadian law, is responsible to deliver and implement security plans on their territories, but over 20 organisations and agencies have jurisdictions and access to the port, the integrated plan is coordinated by the port authority and by the Director of Security and Fire Prevention. The Royal Canadian Mounted Police set up National Port Enforcement Team (NPETs) in key Canadian ports. Dedicated RCMP officers are assigned to the Port of Montreal, and they work in close cooperation with other agencies such as the City of Montreal Police (SPVM), Sûreté du Québec and Canada Border Services Agency (CBSA).

77During the course of this project, the following authorities were approached: Royal Canadian Mounted Police (Port Enforcement & Organised Crime); City of Montreal Police, Organised Crime; Sûreté du Quebec, Organised Crime; Authority for Public Contracts Quebec; Port of Montreal Security Unit; Canadian Border Services Authority Union, International Longshoremen Association, Checkers; Commission of Inquiry on the Awarding and Management of Public Contracts in the Construction Industry (Charbonneau Commission, former prosecutor); Anti-Corruption Permanent Unit (UPAC).

Illicit Trafficking
Drug trafficking

Public Safety Canada hosted a Law Enforcement Roundtable on Drugs on March 29, 2019, in Halifax, Nova Scotia, to foster partnerships and shared knowledge on the status of the illicit drug trade in Canada. Two main themes were discussed: the so-called 'opioid crisis' and the upsurge into methamphetamine. Overall trafficking of illicit substances by organised criminal is on the rise in Canada. OCGs are becoming increasingly involved in different drug markets, giving rise to poly-drug trafficking as well as increased trafficking of cocaine, methamphetamine, and fentanyl. With respect to the fentanyl market, the profitability and relative ease of entry into Canada attracts OCGs, leading to greater supply. The Roundtable noticed the increasing adaptability of criminal networks to detection and interdiction efforts and develop alternative transportation and concealment methods. Specifically, the Roundtable found that OCGs originating in Mexico have been increasingly involved in the trafficking of illicit drugs, including methamphetamines and opioids, to North America. Consequently, drug enforcement efforts in both Canada and the United States must continuously evolve. The routes from Latin America to Canada challenge border security in the United States, with cartels diversifying their products and *"**fractionalising** their organisation to avoid disruption and dismantlement"*[77]. These criminal enterprises exploit air, maritime and land-based transportation domains to smuggle and distribute illicit substances, including cocaine, heroin, and methamphetamine.

---

[77] Public Safety Canada 2019 Law Enforcement Roundtable on Drugs, Meeting Summary, September 2019, page 5

The port of Montreal has a reputation of Canada's drug-smuggling hub; this is due to the volume of trade in the port as much as it is linked to the prolific organised crime scene of the city of Montreal. While open statistics from CBSA are not broken down by port and regional seizures, to the rise in business for the docks of Montreal seems to correspond a rise in illicit trade as well. Between 2016 and 2018 trends for the city of Montreal and the province show the rise of cocaine and heroin consumption, as much as upsurge in meth consumption and the steady, widespread use of cannabis and hashish.

Drug trafficking in the port of Montreal seems to be linked to balance in the underworld of the city of Montreal. In particular, in a city of over a million and half people, **organised crime groups of different factions seem to be working together** to exploit various venues of profit without much conflict. Notwithstanding their collaboration, the Furthermore, with drugs, the main sponsors of the importations are notoriously the same players in town. What might change are their **facilitators**, those with contacts in the country of origin for the drugs. They will work for different groups and will decide whether to use the port, if they have a safe **door of entry**.

An operation that shows this mechanism is **Project Celsius** in 2010-2012, with cases in court until 2018. Project Celsius led to seizures for a total of 43.3 tonnes of hashish, made from the nine containers that were intercepted, the seizures made prior to Project Celsius and the other seizures made during the course of the investigation. The drugs had an estimated value of $860 million and *"could have supplied every resident of a city of 10,000 with a daily dose for more than 11 years"* [78].

Celsius was led by the Montréal RCMP Drug Section jointly with the Montréal and Halifax RCMP National Ports Enforcement Teams and initiated after the Canada Border Services Agency (CBSA) found hashish in offshore containers at the ports of Montreal and Halifax in 2009 and 2010. According to the press release on Celsius, the involved criminal organisation purchased drugs from the Middle East, primarily from Pakistan. The hashish was hidden in containers that were shipped by boat and transited through several ports before being routed to Canada. Some of the suspicious containers were seized in Pakistan, while others were intercepted on their way to Canada, specifically in Italy and Belgium.

The criminal organisation was made of 9 people in Quebec, charged for conspiracy, importation and possession of cannabis resin for the purpose of trafficking. Also 2 people were arrested in Pakistan as leaders of the organization there. The network's **modus operandi** in Montreal was as follows: when a suspicious container arrived in Montréal, a fax was sent to a local hotel. One of the suspects picked up the fax and implemented a plan to take possession of the container. Various details of these contacts led investigators to believe that **employees** performing

---

[78] https://www.canadainternational.gc.ca/italy-italie/media/rcmp_seizure-grc_saisie.aspx?lang=eng

various duties with companies at the Port of Montreal Terminal Cast could be involved in the organisation.

Among those arrested two are particularly interesting for this project: Alain Charron and Brian Forget. Charron was sentenced in 2018 to a five-year prison term for bringing three large shipments of hashish into Canada in 2010[79]. He run meetings with almost all of the major organised crime groups based in Montreal – from the Hells Angels to the Rizzuto clan (Italian mafia), including famous underworld figure Raynald Desjardins, considered the head of the Montreal mafia.

> ✱ The involvement of **different crime groups** working with the same drug broker and the interdependency among the various players in the drug conspiracy are characteristic of this case and are representative of Montreal underworld.

The importations were also aided by the proximity with the **West End Gang**, the group that is historically linked to the **Matticks** family and Irish-based networks that authorities consider highly embedded in the docks in Montreal. **Brian Forget** - a member of the West End Gang sentenced to five-year sentence in 2013 – was considered the middle man between Charron and employees of the Port of Montreal. Thanks to his connections to the port, Forget had the necessary connections

---

[79] R. c. Charron 2018 QCCS 1382; R. c. Charron 2018 QCCS 1770; R. c. Charron 2018 QCCS 2508;

to facilitate the entry of illegal drugs into Canada. The use of intermediaries like Forget served as an insulating device for the key players, said the court; intermediaries were used as buffers for the principal players.

> ★ Obviously, the importation of drugs into Canada requires a «**door**» or a safe port of entry. The door could be someone working in the inside as a baggage handler at the airport of Montreal or a **longshoreman** working at the port of Montreal.

A spin off of this story was the case of **Brenda Forget against Transport Canada**[80]. Mrs Forget lost her job as a checker[81] at the port of Montreal (a job she had since 2005) once her security clearance to have access to certain areas in the port of Montreal was revoked. The revocation of Mrs Forget's security clearance was largely a result of her "association" with her brother, Brian Forget. While Mrs Forget claimed against discrimination for her family status, the RCMP had sent a report in support of the revocation. From the report the court learned that Mrs Forget's name had appeared as a person of interest in a number of police reports about organised crime in the Port of Montreal, due to

---

[80] Forget v. Canada (Transport), 2017 FC 620

[81] in French they call them vérificateurs. They have what they call a stow plan, which is a document that says exactly what will be coming off a boat, and this way they'll know exactly which container must go to which place and they will have these containers placed in a stack to move them with transport of any kind.

her association with Brian Forget. She had also been charged (and charged dismissed) in 2005 after large volumes of cannabis were found in her house and the police also considered her directly involved in, and/or direct knowledge of, the transportation of stolen goods through the Port of Montreal. The Office for Reconsideration she appealed to, however, found that her connection to her brother was not considered problematic to the point of justifying the revocation of security clearance, nor did the police suspicions. However, the Office maintained the revocation of the security clearance because Mrs Forget's guardianship over her niece (Brian's daughter) makes her a potential target who could be suborned to assist her brother, putting the security of marine transportation in jeopardy. Finally, the court quashed this decision and allowed judicial review in favour of Mrs Forget as the standard of reasonable suspicions was eventually not met.

- ✶ The complexities of **family relationships** that seem to bind together **dockworkers** is a constant of various ports. In Montreal, this also creates tensions with security clearance measures, because of difficult balances with guilt by association presumptions.

What else can we learn from the drug trade and importation in Montreal?

A. There is a tendency to **compartmentalise** organised crime in the city of Montreal, differentiating groups, leaderships and coordination structures. **Ethnicity** of origin (of the group, rather than of individuals) remain crucial in understanding ties, even when it is clear **groups work together** as needed, the heads meet when there is a problem. The West End Gang – i.e. the Irish 'mafia' – remains notoriously associated to the port, even though there is considerable proof that they lost ground. Many operations have targeted specific groups: Project Printemps in 2001 and Sharq in 2009 against the Hells Angels; Project Boeuf against the West End Gang in 2002; Project Colisee in 2006 against the Italian mafia; and Project Magot-Mastiff in 2015-2016 against the various heads of the different groups, including Italian mafia.

B. Even though no-one really 'controls' the port, individuals close to **Italian organised crime** seem to have imposed themselves and gained enough authority over other groups active on the port – including individuals close to the so-called West End Gang of Irish-descent. As containers are less and less likely to be opened in the port, all is needed are 2 or 3 people who check on the container for a couple of days or as long as needed and make sure that the container goes on the right truck. Whoever wants to use the port needs to **pay for access** to known characters close to Italian organised crime and the West End Gang. They can 1) **offer information** on how the dock works on a daily basis and 2) control the **smoothness** of the operation as said above. Failure to do so might result in consequent intimidation and retribution.

C. In all of these projects, **corruption of border or customs agents** at the port (and at the airport) or **involvement of dock workers** was one of the doors to bring in cocaine and cannabis into Montreal, among other mechanisms of smuggling (via plane or truck). In Colisee, for example, the organisation was found to have *"the services of a corrupt customs officer providing them with pre-stamped customs declaration cards and customs codes, all to ensure the transportation of narcotics by human couriers"*[82].

D. From the port perspective importations are an open business, anyone with a 'door' can use the port for 'new jobs'. From the city perspective, drug importations especially **cocaine**, are more difficult for newcomers. Cocaine trafficking and importation offences have increased of 7% in 2018[83]. It is a free market but it's controlled by a couple of individuals who have **influence** over some key markets. This is because, whereas importation is up to whoever has the money to finance it

---

[82] Cour Du Québec Sa Majesté La Reine V Arcadi, Francesco Del Balso, Francesco Giordano, Lorenzo Renda, Paolo Rizzuto, Nicolo Sollecito, Rocco, 18.09.2008, Projet Colisée- Aperçu De La Preuve – Sentence, p.8
[83] https://www150.statcan.gc.ca/n1/pub/85-002-x/2019001/article/00013-eng.htm

and the door to import it, **distribution** is more controlled by the various groups in the city, through a couple of influential key figures.

E. Availability of **cocaine** in the city has increased, but port seizures and the centrality of port in general for importation have decreased. The quality of cocaine is higher (over 85% purity, when brought by 'reliable' importers, so that it can be cut afterwards and arrive 20/30% purity on the street).

F. When law enforcement attempts disrupt and dismantle routes or criminal groups who were using the port, by **affecting their modus operandi**, there is an expectation that another modus operandi will emerge, but it might not be about the port anymore. In particular, not all groups in Montreal will use the port of Montreal, as much as groups who might use the port of Montreal (as they have a door there) might not be from Montreal. A group based in Montreal might find it easier and safer to try a 'door' in Vancouver and move drugs from Vancouver to Montreal on the road. This is also why, for border protection federal police teams, **intelligence** (about containers and their movements cross borders) is run **centrally** in Ottawa and disseminated across the various states and provinces separately.

G. In Montreal, there are two main scenarios to import drugs, especially cocaine, equally available, depending on how much money is there for the importation and how much risk the importer is willing to take.

1. **Scenario no.1** - dubbed by analysts, the **'pizza delivery'** scenario. This is more likely to happen with brokers who are in direct contact with traffickers, from Colombia and from Mexico for example, who can bear the risk of the delivery themselves. In this case, the cost of the delivery increases as the traffickers and the brokers handle all the logistics and the risks of finding the 'door' to smuggle the drugs in. The importers need to pay for the whole 'job', including delivery costs, usually for at least a half of the total upfront.

2. **Scenario no.2** – dubbed by analysis the **'pizza collection'** scenario. In this scenario, the financiers of the job will pay brokers expenses, but the collection is handled by someone else and therefore the risk is handled differently by the financiers. In this case the payment might be after collection, if the financiers are strong enough and worried that the collection might not be safe.

Other illicit trade

As noticed by a report from 2011 for Public Safety Canada[84] escalation in the manufacture, importation, and distribution of counterfeit consumer products internationally in recent years has also impacted Canada. Vancouver port seems to be more affected than Montreal in this case, due to the proximity with China and South-East Asia were most of this traffic seems to originate. In Canada, generally, like illegal drugs and precursor chemicals, shipping containers are used to smuggle large quantities of **counterfeit articles**, including contraband cigarettes and multiple other consumer products (from pharmaceuticals, to clothing, to brands).

Like in other ports, also in Montreal there is concern over **illegal waste disposal and trafficking**, mostly to Western Africa. Outbound checks are confirmed to be virtually non-existent. Toxic waste, e-waste and other un-declared waste are problematic to detect in containers, notwithstanding the technical capacities available. As noticed by the Port Authority, this also relates to the capability that technology has to identify risk cargo in this field. In fact, available **technology** cannot penetrate the dense substances (such as concrete and tungsten) used to contain and shield nuclear or radiological materials.

---

[84] Presidia Security Consulting (2011) Economic sectors vulnerable to organized crime: marine port operations. Prepared for Research and National Coordination Organized Crime Division Law Enforcement and Policing Branch Public Safety Canada, Ottawa

Radiation-based technology cannot be used to scan food, plant or animal cargo.

Among the topics discussed in the course of this project two other illicit trades through the port of Montreal have been flagged as interesting, both **outbound**: auto/vehicles theft and shipment; and food products frauds and shipments. This, obviously, does not mean that other 'traditional' illicit trades, such as counterfeit goods or tobacco are not of interest for this port and its authorities; rather their incidence in the last years has been on trend with other countries' experiences.

I. **Auto/vehicles theft/shipment:** this relates to the outbound shipment, via containers, of stolen cars or other vehicles destined usually to African or Middle Eastern destinations. It is usually a trade-based money laundering scheme involving the purchase of used cars and other vehicles for shipment and sale abroad, with funds provided by banks, currency exchanges, and individuals associated with a variety of organised criminal groups. According to the Insurance Bureau of Canada, a car is stolen every 6 minutes in Canada and auto theft has been on the rise[85], even though police-reported motor vehicle theft rates have been stable between 2018-2019[86].

---

[85] http://www.ibc.ca/on/auto/theft
[86] https://www150.statcan.gc.ca/n1/pub/85-002-x/2019001/article/00013-eng.htm

The CBSA warns that the shipment of stolen cars, or boats, or other vehicles remains a priority. But it is underestimated by law enforcement agencies. Without quick police investigations on the networks behind those shipment and without confirmation that the cars have been indeed stolen, it is difficult to hold the vehicles and avoid their shipment altogether. There is indeed a problem with investigating this type of criminality as competence of police forces in this field is unclear (between federal and state) and resources to investigate crimes who also are unlikely to result in a clear sentence are scarce. This type of illicit trade requires forged documents and stolen identity of existing import/export companies to register fraudulently the luxury vehicles and export them to Africa (usually via Europe, primarily Italy and Belgium) or Middle East and Asian countries (usually through Vancouver or North American ports). Behind these criminal activities are a variety of criminal networks, some of whom are linked to Russian-speaking and Eastern European organised crime groups, even though the majority remain local offenders.

II. **Food products fraud and shipment**: this relates to (low/inferior quality) food products that are shipped by means of fraudulent activities. The following scenario has been offered as an example of such fraudulent activity, involving multiple layers of illicit gains:

a. A front man for an organised crime figure in Montreal buys good quality chicken in the USA, spending less than they would in Canada.
b. When they bring it to the border, they pay duties on it; they then show paperwork to demonstrate that the chickens are going to be exported outside of Canada, only passing through the Port of Montreal and then going to Africa. Thus, taxes and duties are reimbursed.
c. The good quality chicken is sold in Canada through a black-market network, in restaurants or supermarkets.
d. Garbage pieces of chickens or other low quality/cheaper chickens are shipped to the initially declared Africa destination where other profit is secured by previously arranged brokerage.

The main fraudulent activity here is considered to be **tax and duty evasion**, even though there are a number of other chained activities also illegal that could potentially amount to white collar or even corporate kind of criminality.

Infiltration in the legal economy, corruption and governance issues

Aside from the examples of corruption that were described above as enablers of illicit trade, **corruption** in the port of Montreal, as **tool and manifestation of organised crime infiltration**, has been flagged up in various occasions during this project as an ongoing and systemic concern for the Port of Montreal. In particular, conversations related to the known involvement of some longshoremen and checkers in the commission of criminal activities by organised crime groups, as well as to the involvement of some customs and border agents as well. While criminal involvement and responsibilities remain an individual choice, the port system overall is deemed to be criminogenic. A report by Senate Standing Committee on National Security and Defence[87] in 2007 reported that

"It is about time to get serious about the degree of corruption and vulnerability at our seaports. There seems to be a level of comfort among labour unions, the business community and port authorities with the way things are done now.
None of them seem anxious to reform a system that is currently providing plenty of income for everyone – including crooks. All those people should wake up to the fact that their house of cards is likely to come tumbling down if one nasty container gets through. The Committee is convinced that all

---

[87] Canadian Security Guide Book (2007) An Update of Security Problems in Search of Solutions – SEAPORTS Standing Senate Committee on National Security and Defence

workers at Canada's seaports should require security clearances".

The Senate Standing Committee on National Security and Defence, in 2002[88], reported on police estimates: at the port of Montreal, 15% of stevedores had criminal records, as did 36.3% of "checkers," who go over manifest lists for cargo containers, and fully 54% of the employees of a company with the contract to pick up garbage, do minor repairs and operate the tenders servicing ships moored in open water outside the harbour. The committee reported that the union that supplies dockworkers appeared closed to outsiders; applicants must be sponsored by current union members, "who are sometimes members of crime families and their friends," the report states.

The Port of Montreal now requires that truckers with Transport Canada security clearance have their fingerprints scanned upon entry, as the first Canadian port to comply with **Transport Canada's Marine Transportation Security Clearance Program (MTSCP).** In Montreal, the same program applies also to law enforcement at the port including CBSA. The program was introduced since 2004 and generally applies to workers in the marine sector who perform certain duties or have access to

---

[88] https://sencanada.ca/Content/SEN/Committee/371/defe/rep/rep05feb02-e.htm

certain restricted areas[89]. Notwithstanding the curbing on corruption as tool to serve organised crime's interests on the waterfront, there is still **mistrust** towards both customs/border agents and longshoremen/checkers, both from management in the same institutions and from outsiders. The security clearance process is often seen as intrusive from both the longshoremen and the CBSA's perspectives as the level of information collected and then shared might represent yet another vulnerability of the system.

Aside from the attempts to curb corruption as enabler and facilitator of organised crime, Montreal's history with corruption in the legal economy and with systemic forms of collusion as well, gives interesting insights into the possibility of **corruption as autonomous activity** also at the port, for what relates to construction, infrastructure maintenance and obviously services and governance of the port space. In fact, since the Charbonneau Commission published its report in 2015 and UPAC's (Unité Permanente Anti-Corruption) investigations started getting stronger, investigations on corruption and collusion in Montreal have received unprecedented interest. The Charbonneau Commission (officially the **Commission of Inquiry on the Awarding and Management of Public Contracts in the Construction Industry**) was a public inquiry in Quebec (2011-2015) into potential corruption, and organised crime infiltration,

---

[89] https://www.tc.gc.ca/eng/marinesecurity/regulatory-initiatives-infopackagemtscp-197.htm

in the management of public construction contracts. The commission was also set to paint a portrait of activities involving collusion and corruption in the provision and management of public contracts in the construction industry (including private organisations, government enterprises and municipalities) and to include any links with the financing of political parties. UPAC was also established by the government of Quebec in 2011, to coordinate the efforts of six teams, including the Charbonneau Commission. Another effect of the Charbonneu Commission has also been the strengthening of the **Autorité des marchés publics (AMP)** for Quebec and the establishment, in 2014, of the **Bureau de l'inspecteur général de la Ville de Montréal (BIG)**. The two bodies have similar jurisdictions (even though the AMP's one is more extensive) and they both have mandates to oversee the public procurement processes and contracts in Montreal and in Quebec.

During the Charbonneau Commission one of the witnesses, former construction executive Lino Zambito[90], brought evidence of a conspiracy involving **Robert Abdallah** related to his influence (alleged bid-rigging) over the choice of contractors during his time at the City of Montreal. Other allegations were about an agreement to push for Abdallah as

---

[90] Zambito is the former owner of the Infrabec construction firm. He pleaded guilty in 2015 to fraud and offering bribes in connection to a rigged process to build a water-treatment plant in the Montreal bedroom community of Boisbriand. He is better known, however, as a whistle-blower who exposed Quebec's system of corruption.

head of the Port Authority of Montreal. Robert Abdallah was the director-general of the city of Montreal from 2003 to 2006. In 2007, Mr. Abdallah was the Conservative government's favoured candidate to become the president of the Montreal Port Authority. Former prime minister (2006-2015) Stephen Harper's former spokesman, Dimitri Soudas, discussed Mr. Abdallah's candidacy with many people in government in 2007, including the board of directors of the Montreal port, who was the ultimate decision maker on the matter. The board eventually decided for another candidate. There was no interference proven in any court, even though rumours of an RCMP investigation surfaced at the time, but these allegations are problematic for a number of reasons that have to do with the proximity of Abdallah to individuals and companies that were heavily involved in the findings of the Commission. The relevant events and considerations relating to these allegations can be summarised as follow, according to reconstructions from the Charbonneau Commission transcripts, reports[91] and the narratives from some of the participants.

    i.   There is proof that Mr Abdallah has travelled to Barbados, where he also resided, with Mr Tony Accurso – one of the entrepreneurs that in that period (2003-2006) had the highest amount of contracts for public work with the city council with his three main companies. This trip was not an isolated fact, as they also travelled to

---

[91] Rapport de la Commission d'enquête sur l'octroi et la gestion des contrats publics dans l'industrie de la construction, Tome 2, Récit de faits

the Caribbeans and, in 2006, to Las Vegas together with Mr Frank Zampino, the president of the executive committee of the city council. A lot of the expenses in these trips were paid by Mr Accurso, notwithstanding the clear guidance to which Mr Abdallah and Mr Zampino were both subjected, as employees of the City, not to accept any type of present or payment by actors who had any commercial or business dealings with the city. The friendship between Accurso and Abdallah – that consisted of attending each other family gatherings and also travelling together - pre-existed his nomination to the city council, as the two had met in the 1980s when Accurso inherited Construction Louisbourg that had contracts with Hydro-Quebec, managed by Adballah.

ii. After the trip to Vegas in 2006, the mayor Gerald Tremblay is informed of the 'friendship' with Accurso and asks for his resignation. After he quits the city Mr Abdallah becomes president of Gastier MP, one of Accurso's enterprises. This one of various appointments of public managers into companies that had had contracts with the city.

iii. In this context, when Mr Abdallah became a candidate for the port authority job, the influence of Accurso seemed to plausible. An audio recording surfaced purporting to be the voices of Accurso and another Montreal construction executive discussing how Soudas (the prime minister's spokesperson) and his friend Leo Housakos could help get Abdallah appointed in 2007.

Housakos, who is referred to as "Leo" throughout the recording, was appointed to the Senate in 2009, which corresponds to what referred by Zambito to the Commission.

iv. Mr Tony Accurso has been convicted to 4 years in prison in 2018 on five charges[92]: conspiracy to commit acts of corruption, conspiracy to commit fraud, fraud of over $5,000, municipal corruption, and aiding in a breach of trust. Accurso was accused of being part of a system of corruption that eliminated all competition for municipal contracts in Laval (a city at the outskirts of Montreal) between 1996 and 2010. Mr. Accurso's firms were also convicted of tax fraud.

v. Mr Frank Zampino - second-in-command at Montreal city hall from 2002 to 2008 was arrested on corruption and fraud-related charges in 2012 related to the sale of the city-owned land known as Faubourg Contrecoeur, but was acquitted in the case in 2018. He was again arrested in 2017 following a **UPAC-led investigation** into the city's water-meter contract that broadened into an investigation into political financing. Together with Zampino, also Robert Adballah was involved in the UPAC raids, for their alleged involvement in a scheme to hand out municipal contracts to engineering firms in return for political financing, kickbacks and other benefits.

---

[92] Accurso c. R., 2018 QCCA 1144; Accurso c. Charbonneau, 2014 QCCS 2108

To complete this very complex set of facts and series of events, Mr Accurso acknowledged to the Commission having had ties with senior members of the Italian Mafia in Montreal, describing Vito Rizzuto and his son Nick Jr – both deceased and both considered without any doubts as heads of the Montreal Italian mafia – as "minor contacts" in his wide business network. A rival of Mr Accurso in the construction industry said that Accurso was actually using mafia ties whenever he needed any dispute settlement.

The Charbonneau Commission in fact did argue that members of the Rizzuto clan were enlisted to settle disputes among construction companies over contract bids and also collected cash from them. Nick jr Rizzuto was shot in 2009. Vito Rizzuto was subpoenaed to testify at the Charbonneau inquiry, but died of lung cancer in 2013 before he could appear. Operations like Project Colise, which heavily affected the criminal endeavours of the Rizzuto clans and associates, did provide the Commission for a good starting point to essentially understand that a number of enterprises with public contracts in the city of Montreal did have mafia links – they did use **mafia protection** to organise the market and settle unfair competition rules. In particular, and in relation to this project, Vito and his son Nick jr were implicated by the Commission in the construction of **1000 de la Commune**, a project that transformed an old cold-storage warehouse of the Port of Montreal – just outside the fenced part of the port starts in front of the Santi-Laurent river, at the end of the Old Port area – in a series of luxury condos. The Commission found that:

- A number of other entrepreneurs were implicated in the dossiers of 1000 de la Commune. When the SVPM (a federal company, Société du Vieux-Port de Montreal) launched the call for tenders, Construction Gescor and HarbourTeam of brothers **Tony** and **Alberino Magi** win the bid and coordinate with a fiduciary for a necessary warranty on the works. Some financial difficulties delay the works until the fiduciary calls back their guarantees.
- Another entrepreneur, Mike Argento, offers to help the Magis, by involving the Rizzuto family. Vito Rizzuto uses his contacts and facilitators in the financial services and in particular Jonathan Myette. They agree to help Magi with the project and get half of its revenue afterwards. Rizzuto agrees to act as the **enforcer** against Magi to make sure he falls in line. This is 2002.
- In 2007 a unit of the building was bought by one of the companies of entrepreneur Giuseppe Borsellino to resell it in 2010.
- In between 2007 and 2010 the property was shared with the director of FTQ-Construction who was also sharing the business with **Raynald Desjardins**, a very notorious organised crime member, close to the Rizzuto as much as other criminal groups in the city, including the Hells Angels.
- Desjardins was given an apartment and a garage in the building without paying anything for it.
- When in 2009 Borsellino is assaulted by three strangers at one of his companies, that was a message delivered by

people close to Desjardins and the Rizzuto: the **intimidation** message was to have the entrepreneur keep quiet about the nature of the business that – he had learned – was ongoing in that building.
- **Tony Magi was killed** at the beginning of 2019. It was not the first attempt to his life (as he had been hospitalised in 2008 following a shooting). He had entered in business with Nick Rizzuto Jr over a construction project before Nick Jr was killed in 2009 near Magi's company. Magi was rumoured to have played a part in Nick Jr's murder. There is an attempt to Magi's wife's life in 2011 alongside different problems to people working for him. When in 2019 he is killed no one is surprised as newspaper link the events to the proximity, and animosity with the Rizzutos.

Research notes and emerging themes

The following themes have emerged from research fieldwork and notes as deserving of further attention and scrutiny, in no particular order:

A. The drug trade through the port of Montreal does not necessarily mirror the drug trade in the city of Montreal: **other ports**, such as Halifax or even Vancouver or New York are often preferred to Montreal.
B. The **modus operandi** of a criminal group will determine which is the most important person for a drug importation, through the port or in other ways. This will

be the person holding the most crucial **function** with a degree of **discretionary power**. The criminal analyst needs to be able to see which organisation is using which person that could also be used by other organisations as providing a door.
C. The increase use of **other methods to ship illicit products**, including drugs, precursors and pharmaceuticals into Quebec and Montreal have brought to a decrease of the use of containership for illegal trades. Other methods of shipment include boats, smaller vessels, yachts, postal/courier systems (which seem also liked to an increase in the use of online drug resellers through the dark web).
D. The port is considered **unreliable** by criminal groups, as the risks associated to losing the shipment, having the container intercepted or delayed are to high. Security measures, as in other ports, seem to have had a **displacement** effect on the methods of drug supply.
E. Leveraging the **dark web** and postal/courier systems for trafficking of illicit substances has created numerous challenges for supply reduction and interdiction efforts, which seems to have taken away the focus from the port.
F. CBSA thoroughly inspects about **three per cent of containers** that roll through the port. Even when screening devices scan each container, there is a limit in the type of commodities they can identify. Inspections are only done when intelligence suggests something is wrong with the container and there is a very high

likelihood, if not certainty, that the containers carries illicit substances.
G. Canada **legalised** the use of **cannabis** in 2018; it is too early to judge the full extent of the changes in the market. However, the trends confirm that the black market is still ongoing, as criminal groups operate by undercutting government's supply and taxes. The price of cannabis, overall has gone down.
H. The legacy of the Charbonneau Commission and the current works of the UPAC has left a profound scar in the trust system of the city of Montreal. With new **plans** for the port of Montreal to **expand** beyond the territory of Contrecoeur, the level of attention by the different authorities overseeing the allocation of contracts remain unusually high

Case Study 4
New York & New Jersey, USA

Photo: Port Elizabeth, August 2019, Author's rights

General information

The Port of New York and New Jersey runs across 40 km (across 17 counties) along the New York–New Jersey Harbour Estuary, which runs along 1,050 km of shoreline in the vicinity of New York City and north-eastern New Jersey. It is the busiest port of the East Coast and third of the USA for tonnage, following only Los Angeles and Long Beach, in California.

New York Harbour has six container terminals in New York City (Staten Island and Brooklyn), Jersey City, Newark and Elizabeth. With 34 terminals[93] and 7,1 million TEUs (2018)[94], the port is the busiest containership of the East Coast. The port receives the most first port of calls, 72%, more than any other East Coast port. Its most relevant partner is China (27% of trade), followed by India, Germany and Italy. Even though commonly associated to the city of New York, the majority of trade in the port is actually in New Jersey and especially in Port Elizabeth. The decline of business in Brooklyn and Staten Island – since the 1980s - has been associated to geographical conditions – i.e. the capability of other terminals to receive larger and deeper ships – as well as investments in the development of infrastructures and political choices by the Port Authority. According to its website, enterprises involved with the port support 400,000 jobs representing nearly $25.7 billion in annual wages. Meanwhile

---

[93] https://www.panynj.gov/port/temperature-controlled-cargo.html
[94] https://www.panynj.gov/port/pdf/trade-statistics-2018.pdf

the port generates close to $8.5 billion in federal, state and local tax revenues[95].

There are six container terminals in NY/NJ port. The port is a landlord port run by Port Newark Container Terminal, Maher Terminals and APM Terminals in Port Elizabeth, GCT New York LP Terminals in Staten Island, GCT Bayonne LP Terminals in Jersey City and Red Hook Container Terminals in Brooklyn.[96] Over the Hudson River it was not always easy to manage the jurisdiction of land and water between the two states of New York and New Jersey on which the estuary is naturally located. In 1921, with the creation of the Port of New York Authority, the port district became a bi-state business.

Policing and Security Authorities

All levels of government and private companies are responsible for different activities and areas of the port. The Port Authority – which is also responsible for the region's airport and other real estate (i.e. World Trade Centre) – has its own police force and an inspector general office. The port police of the Port Authority - overseen by the Office of the Inspector general – is responsible for daily security at New York Harbour, where each terminal implements their own security protocols as well. Other agencies, such as the US Coast Guard, the Waterfront Commission, US Customs and Border Protection and US

---

[95] https://www.panynj.gov/port/en/our-port/facts-and-figures.html
[96] https://www.panynj.gov/port/containerized-cargo.html

Immigration and Customs Enforcement regulate access of goods and people, while New York Police Department, Federal Bureau of Investigations and Drug Enforcement Administration all have ad-hoc access to the terminals when needed during their policing operations. In particular, US Customs and Border Protection is tasked with the integration of security into the commercial operations of the port. For the purposes of this research the following authorities have been involved: the Waterfront Commission of New York Harbour (field visits and 2 collective interviews); Federal Bureau of Investigations-NY field office, (Transnational Organised Crime, 1 collective interview); Drug Enforcement Administration-NY (1 collective interview); New York Police Department (Criminal Enterprise Unit, 1 focus group); Port Authority of NY and NJ (Office of the Inspector General, 1 collective interview); US Customs and Border Protection-NY and NJ (1 focus groups with field visit); New Jersey Police Department, Homeland Security (NJ-Transnational Organised Crime, 1 focus group with field visit).

Illicit Trafficking

Drug Trafficking

In the past couple of years, the trends of drug seizures in the US overall show important rises. According to overall figures by U.S. Customs and Border Protection's (CBP) Air and Marine Operations (AMO), in Fiscal Year 2019, enforcement actions resulted in the seizure or disruption of 284,825 pounds of cocaine, 101,874 pounds of marijuana, and 51,058 pounds of methamphetamine. The Drug Enforcement Agency (DEA), in their 2019[97] national drug threat assessment, indicates that the availability of cocaine is high in NY and it has increased since 2017-2018[98] when it was marked as moderate and stable. High – but not noticeably growing - is also the availability of marijuana; moderate and growing is the availability of Psychoactive Substances; high and worryingly growing is the availability of fentanyl; high and stable is the availability of heroin; moderate and stable is methamphetamine. The DEA report in both 2018 and 2019 analyse the networks and the distribution of illicit drugs across the US. In a city like New York this analysis is done by starting from the commodities and then understanding the groups behind it and their modus operandi. The DEA's reflections on how the drug trade has developed in NYC can be summarised as follows:

- All NYC-based gangs (Bloods, subsets of the Bloods – the city's predominant gangs, MS-13, Trinitarios, Crips, and Latin Kings) traffic all available drugs, primarily marijuana, cocaine, and heroin, and to a lesser extent, Controlled Prescription Drugs (CPDs).
- Of the various criminal enterprises involved in the importation of drugs from **Mexico**, the Jalisco New

---

[97] https://www.dea.gov/sites/default/files/2020-01/2019-NDTA-final-01-14-2020_Low_Web-DIR-007-20_2019.pdf
[98]

Generation Cartel (CJNG) - based in the city of Guadalajara in the Mexican State of Jalisco - is the most recently formed and is particularly active in NYC, together with other cartels (i.e. Los Zetas, Juarez).

- Authorities have noticed the **Dominican criminal groups dominate the mid-level distribution of cocaine and white powder heroin** in major drug markets mainly in the Northeast United States, and control the wholesale distribution of heroin and fentanyl in certain areas. They also engage in street-level sales in select parts of the region. Illegal drugs destined for Dominican groups in the Northeast primarily arrive first in New York City, where the drugs are distributed throughout the greater metropolitan area, or routed to secondary hubs and retail markets in other regions. Dominican groups work in collaboration with foreign suppliers to have cocaine, heroin, and fentanyl shipped directly to the Northeast from Mexico, Colombia, and the Dominican Republic. They are sourcing their fentanyl from Mexican traffickers, expanding the reach of both organizations.

- As **cocaine production** in Colombia has resurged, increasing of almost 400% in the last 4-5 years, **Colombian groups** remain leaders in production and trafficking of cocaine. Cocaine is generally transported and stored in large quantities in remote areas of Venezuela and Ecuador until maritime or aerial transportation can be secured and shipments can proceed to Mexico, Central America, and the Caribbean.

- The overall increased availability of cocaine in the United States might have led, in NYC, to a significant co-occurrence of cocaine and **fentanyl** in overdose deaths.
- The importation of these drugs to NYC differs in origin, network and obviously method of shipment. **Smuggling techniques** mostly include movement and concealment in vehicles, but also have included underground tunnels, maritime and air means, including speedboats, fishing vessels, semi-submersibles, private aircraft, and commercial air and sea cargo. Maritime importation, including commercial cargos through seaports, is still particularly frequent for cocaine.

In 2018 546.5 lbs of cocaine have been seized in the port, according to the CBP. Dubbed as the **second largest seizure of its kind in 25 years**, on February 28 2019, approximately 3,200 lbs of cocaine (approximately 1.5 tons), with an estimated street value of $77,000,000, was seized at the Port of New York/Newark in a joint operation involving U. S. Customs and Border Protection (CBP), the U. S. Coast Guard (USCG), Homeland Security Investigations (HSI), the Drug Enforcement Administration (DEA), the New York Police Department (NYPD), and the New York State Police (NYSP). The shipment, just arrived from Colombia, was intercepted when the vessel, MSC Carlotta, stopped over in New York/Newark on its way to Antwerp, Belgium. It contained a legitimate shipment of dried fruit, whose seal looked like it had been tampered with. It is unclear whether the drugs were destined for the U.S., or meant to continue on to

Europe. According to the authorities involved, this seizure was one of the confirmative events that cocaine is back in large quantities on the streets of NYC and that what authorities can seize is a small portion of all the available cocaine. In fact, from NYC field office of the DEA start various investigations that lead to seizure elsewhere. Drugs might not seem to reach the port of NY/NJ but they do reach the city when smuggled through another entry point. For example, in June 2019, 16 tons of cocaine where seized in the **port of Philapdephia** carried by MSC Gayane, a 1,030-foot Liberian-flagged container ship. The intelligence on that shipment had been released from NYC offices.

What else can we learn from the drug trade and importation in New York/New Jersey?

A. Traffickers seem to push to build an **emerging customer base of users mixing cocaine with fentanyl.** Even though fentanyl's – an opioid - potent deadly effect (2 milligrams) might however discourage some cocaine users, it might 'hook' others and decrease the price of some cocaine on the market, boosting competition. Or it might just be a mistake done by the dealers for lack of hygiene when cutting their drugs. Not just cocaine, but also and primarily heroin is often cut with fentanyl to make it more potent, which has been a leading factor in **America's opioid overdose epidemic**. Indeed, the presence of fentanyl in the New York City drug supply has dramatically increased the number of overdose deaths, and fentanyl is now the most common drug involved in overdose deaths[99]. This might lead to high risk consumptions for occasional users not used to the substance in the first place. A public campaign across the city is still currently active[100].

B. There are still big players controlling some drug markets in the metropolitan area, but things have changed in terms of how the trades are managed. Trading in heroin is usually for capital accumulation, while cocaine is considered the stable business.

C. A typical cocaine trafficker in NYC who used to receive 1 kg of cocaine is now receiving 5 kgs - they all receive more than before. Everyone has jumped up on the supply chain. This is due to the **increased availability of cocaine** from producing countries. Additionally, the financers could be anywhere and not in NYC.

D. In NYC, differently from cities like Montreal, **Mexican cartels' brokers** are said to control the importation – in terms of **methods of transportation** - of cocaine; they

---

[99] https://www1.nyc.gov/site/doh/health/health-topics/fentanyl.page
[100] https://www1.nyc.gov/assets/doh/downloads/pdf/mental/fentanyl-poster.pdf and
https://www1.nyc.gov/assets/doh/downloads/pdf/mental/know-about-fetanyl.pdf

can talk to any other organisation, including Colombian producers and Dominican distributors in the city. Other organisations get bulk drugs and then they distribute in their communities and networks. **Distribution** seems to remain **ethnic-based**.

E. **Chinese and Asian-based groups** are involved in the management of proceeds of crime as they offer a guarantee system of money laundering to the traffickers. The traffickers receive its laundered money (with an increased charge for the risk) even in case of police seizures. This creates an **insulation** between the dealers and the traffickers and offers producers (e.g. in Colombia) to outsource the task of collecting money from the various traffickers too. This system is done mostly in NYC, but also for trafficking happening elsewhere, as NYC is the Mecca for the different aspects of the drug trade.

F. LCN is still active in NYC – mostly beyond drugs. Young smart graduates of the different families, when it comes to drug, do the business like everyone else does it, including use of online technologies. **Italian-American organised crime** individuals are known to handle well the logistics of the drug trade. They have people that help divert things, they are involved with giving people access to different trades as their knowledge and reputation in the city remains superior to many other 'newer' groups.

G. The **volume of cargo** through all the ports in the US is obviously huge and also from NY, there are so many leads on a single day that it becomes easy for importers to organise **diversions** and send authorities in the wrong directions.
H. The links with **Canada** and also Canadian ports and Canadian mailing system even, which is more relaxed for trade relationships, is growing as a concern for what relates to the smuggling of the majority of drugs from Latin America. For example, smaller vessels can depart from Colombia to Puerto Rico or the Dominican Republic, enter Mexico and cross over the border from Mexico to the US and proceed into Canada that way so the US receives trafficking/imports from Canada too to certain extents.
I. When a container is hijacked and it is shipped by a legitimate company, it is quite intricate to understand where is the **criminal organisation behind** that shipment as there will be someone owning the business, more or less aware of the illicit trade, and someone financing the shipment, more or less in touch with the owner of the trade. The system is highly adaptable.

Other illicit trade and the role of CBP

The CBP is responsible for the port of NY/NJ territorially. This is to avoid also confusion over policing and security responsibility. The more one scrutinises the port the more costs for legitimate businesses increase and the more crime gets displaced as observed also in other ports. The merging of US Customs and Border Protection (CBP) into the United State Department of Homeland Security on 1 March 2003 was one among many reactions by the US government to improve national security post 9/11. This change in organisational structure led to a change in the role of CBP.

Most of the other illicit trades are approached from a **fee-collection perspective**, to avoid loss of revenues and duties. As it can take up to 8-10 hours to inspect a container, and obviously depending of what is found in the container (money, guns, drugs, counterfeit...), different agencies might compete to handle the cargo and detain the products (especially if it's cash). CBP utilises predictive analysis, available technology, targeted enforcement, and the ability to rapidly readjust counter surveillance activities to affect and degrade the ability of criminal organisations to operate in a given environment.

In the 9/11 aftermath one of the actions taken, the 9/11 Commission Act, came into force on 3 August 2007. According to Section 1701, Container Scanning and Seals, under the Title XVII, Maritime Cargo of Public Law 110–53—AUG. 3, 2007 issued by the 110th Congress of the US on Implementing Recommendations of the 9/11 Commission Act of 2007, *"A container that was loaded on a vessel in a foreign port shall not enter the United States (either directly or via a foreign port) unless the container was scanned by nonintrusive imaging equipment and radiation detection equipment at a foreign port before it was loaded on a vessel by July 2012".*

In October 2009, the **US Government Accountability Office (GAO)**[101] reported challenges to scanning 100 percent of U.S.- bound cargo at foreign ports. Department of Homeland Security (DHS) officials acknowledged that most, if not all foreign ports, would not be able to meet the July 2012 target date and a viable solution to meet the requirement was difficult to identify.

In September 2013, GAO reported that CBP had not regularly assessed foreign ports for risks to cargo since 2005. GAO recommended that DHS periodically assess the security risks from ports that ship cargo to the United States and use the results to inform whether changes need to be made to **Container Security Initiative** (CSI) ports. CSI is a bilateral government partnership program operated by CBP that aims to identify and examine U.S.-bound cargo container shipments that are at risk of containing Weapons of Mass Destruction or other contraband. As part of the program, CBP officers are stationed at select foreign seaports and review information about US-bound containerised cargo shipments. CBP estimates that, through the CSI program, it pre-screens over 80 percent of all maritime containerised cargo imported into the United States.

In January 2015[102], GAO found that CBP did not have accurate data on the number and disposition of each high-risk shipment scheduled to arrive in the United States. Specifically,

---

[101] https://www.gao.gov/products/gao-16-790t
[102] https://www.gao.gov/assets/680/678249.pdf

CBP's data overstated the number of high-risk shipments, including those that appeared not to be examined or waived in accordance with CBP policy. CBP officers inconsistently applied criteria to make some waiver decisions and incorrectly documented waiver reasons. GAO recommended that CBP define waiver categories and disseminate policy on issuing waivers. In response, CBP issued a new policy that includes **new criteria for waiving examinations of high-risk shipments** and developed a new process for recording waivers and issued a memorandum.

Overall, CBP, since its renewed mandate, has made substantial progress in implementing various initiatives and programs that, collectively, have enhanced cargo security, but some challenges remain. Examples of progress and challenges are generally in the areas of

1. using information for improving targeting and risk assessment of cargo shipments
2. partnerships with foreign governments
3. partnerships with the trade industry.

When it comes to other illicit trade beyond drugs, NY/NJ seems to behave like other ports. As for some other ports elsewhere, **internal conspiracy** is the name for 'organised crime' at play in the port. For internal conspiracy, rip or whip loads, smaller bags concealing illicit goods, are usually the key findings for customs, but larger loads have been more frequent. While rip loads are easier to handle also for CBP, it is often the case that deep concealments will require deeper inspections in the warehouses.

There were 137 seizures in 2018 from commercial vessels, and more than half of them were counterfeit products, in violation of **intellectual property rights**. Prohibited pharmaceuticals are usually sent through airmail but obviously some also come through more vessels. Prohibited firearms, and trafficked art as well might come through maritime routes. Also, like in other ports, agriculture enforcement regulations have caught garbage and environmental violations, also qualifying as waste trafficking and wildlife trafficking at times. The two most common methods of **illegal export** are mislabelling containers to conceal (e)waste and mixing (e)waste with a legitimate consignment, such as end-of- life vehicles, like in NY/NJ in other ports.

In NY/NJ CBP carries out 4 types of inspections: Anti-Terrorism Contraband Enforcement Team (ATCET) Inspection; Non-Intrusive Inspection (NII); Agricultural Inspection: Trade Compliance Inspection. **Automated Targeting System (ATS)** is CBP database of incoming and certain outbound cargo and persons. Advanced screening information is added to the ATS and checked against intelligence data from CBP's National Targeting Center (NTC) and other intelligence and law enforcement databases to produce a risk-based score. Cargo above a certain ATS threshold generally are selected for secondary inspection, but it is unclear how many outbound inspections are carried out in reality. The **Outbound Enforcement Program** is part of CBP's effort to effectively monitor and control the flow of goods and people leaving the United States. Recent figures[103] show that **illicit currencies and drugs** are usually the targets of this program when it comes to cargo. Obviously, CBP the amount of these risk-based Outbound enforcement operations depends on the availability of officers and funding at each port and field division of the CBP.

Infiltration in the legal economy, corruption and governance issues

Differently from other ports, in NY/NJ the most discussed topic during meetings, interviews and collective conversations, has been mostly related to corruption in the port and systemic/endemic manifestations of organised crime related to both the port economy and the port development. This obviously has to do with the spotlight that institutions, such as the Waterfront Commission, has been keeping on certain aspects of the port life in NY/NJ.

In particular three interconnected aspects have emerged in relation to this aspect of the research.

I. The legacy of LCN and the relationship between organised crime and the workforce on the waterfront.

---

[103] https://www.oig.dhs.gov/sites/default/files/assets/2018-02/OIG-18-47-Jan18.pdf

There is a clear indication in the words and in the work of the Waterfront commission that the influence that certain organised crime networks - albeit evolved into different structures from what they were known to be – still persists and still affects the capacity of the port to function in a transparent manner. Also, it is the institutional opinion of the Waterfront commission that the mechanisms of corruption that were known to rule the workforce in the port, through the union (the International Longshoremen Association) have not disappeared, but mainly evolved into more pervasive and hidden forms of corruption and collusion. Various judicial cases collected, even when they are not as contemporary, show these mechanisms at play: these include extortions of union members and, through union members, of companies; loan-sharking to companies and individuals; bogus insurance claims and no-shows job cover up; intimidation. One among various others summarises some of the issues.

📁 US v. Michael Coppola[104].

This case provided evidence of the Genovese family's criminal control over the Manhattan and New Jersey waterfronts generally, and over ILA Local 1235, in particular. Genovese family member George Barone, Genovese associate

---

[104] United States of America, Appellee, v. Michael Coppola, Defendant-Appellant. Docket No. 10-0065-Cr. - United States Court of Appeals, Second Circuit. Argued: May 20, 2011. Decided: February 14, 2012.

Michael D'Urso, Gambino family member Primo Cassarino, and Lucchese family member Thomas Ricciardi testified that criminal "control" over the metropolitan area waterfront dated from the 1950s, with an understanding between the Genovese and Gambino families that the Genoveses would influence and control unions and businesses operating on the Manhattan and New Jersey docks, while the Gambinos would influence and control unions and businesses operating in Brooklyn and Staten Island. When Barone was asked how such control was exercised, he replied, through **"intimidation, fear, whatever"** – the mafia method.

Evidence showed that intimidation and fear was the common method used by the Genovese family to secure and maintain waterfront control. In the Manhattan-based ILA Local 1804-1, control was eventually exercised by Coppola and his one-time Genovese captain, Tino Fiumara who was respected and feared by everyone – as testified by Local 1804-1 vice-president Thomas Buzzanca in the case. The Genovese family used its influence of unions to dictate what businesses worked on the waterfront, by including and excluding any "ordinary guy wanted to go into the trucking business on the docks, or wanted to open up something on the docks", as testified by D'Urso.

Coppola was convicted on a two-count indictment charging him with substantive and conspiratorial racketeering in connection with his activities over three decades as an associate, soldier, and ultimately captain of the Genovese family. The pattern of racketeering through which Coppola was alleged to have conducted and participated in the affairs of the Genovese family was charged in three predicate acts.

Racketeering Act One is particularly interesting; it alleged conspiracy to extort, extortion, and wire fraud in connection with the Genovese family's control of ILA Local 1235. As for the extortion, between January 1974 and March 2007, Coppola and others obtained or conspired to obtain the property of Local 1235 members both in the tangible form of *"Local 1235 labor union positions, money paid as wages and employee benefits and other economic benefits that such Local 1235 union members would have obtained but for the defendant and his co-conspirators' corrupt influence over such union"* and in the intangible form of *"the right of Local 1235 members to have the officers, agents, delegates, employees and other representatives of their labour organisation manage the money, property and financial affairs of the organisation"*. The property was allegedly obtained with the consent of union officials *"induced by wrongful use of actual and threatened force, violence or fear"*.

As to the wire fraud, between January 1974 and March 2007, Coppola and others devised a scheme to defraud Local 1235 union members of (1) the same tangible property charged in the extortion scheme, and (2) intangible property in the form of *"the right of the honest services of the Local 1235 Presidents"*.

In a typical mafia behaviour, the Genovese family was providing *"through contacts (...), **labour peace** on the waterfronts where trucks were picking up containers"*. In exchange for this peace, tribute payments were demanded from both waterfront businesses and unions, based on the earnings that the company and the union made. In addition to monthly tribute payments, the Genovese family demanded **"Christmases"**, special year-end payments. Also, the tributes paid by businesses were often channelled to the criminal enterprise through the union.

With particular reference to Local 1235, evidence from various cases showed Genovese family control of that union for more than thirty years through three successive **local presidents**: Vincent Colucci, Albert Cernadas and Vincent Aulisi. Evidence also showed that the Genovese family exploited its control over waterfront unions to make **union employment decisions**. Barone testified that the Genovese family *"sent word"* to ILA president John Bowers to put Harold Daggett into a senior position with the union. The family then *"told Daggett what we wanted him to do... If he didn't do it, we take him out."* Barone testified that he personally secured union employment for numerous Genovese associates, for example positions at an ILA health care clinic for Coppola's brother and Cernadas' wife, among others. Due to his association with Michael Coppola, Edward Aulisi, a checker working at the Port, and son of former ILA Local 1235 President Vincent Aulisi, was barred from working at any port property since 2009. In 2010, Albert Cernadas, a former president of ILA Local 1235 was arrested on federal charges of racketeering, extortion and conspiracy[105].

What the case against **Cernadas et al.** shows is that in the 30 years before the charges were brought, a continuous mechanism where, for years, these high-ranking members of the ILA did conspire to *"obstruct, delay and affect commerce, and the movement of articles and commodities in commerce, by extortion"*, in that they agreed to obtain money from ILA union members, with their consent induced by wrongful use of actual and threatened force, violence and fear.

> II. *The interests of organised crime and collusive networks over the port economy*

The port economy in NY/NJ is obviously particularly interesting for a number of different reasons that mostly have to do with contracts of services and commerce on the waterfront. In 2007 a civil RICO case against the ILA was filed and still has not been resolved[106]. The case detailed how ILA's president, Harold Daggett, is allegedly an associate of Genovese family part of the "Waterfront Enterprise" - an alleged association-in-fact RICO

---

[105] United States of America v. Stephen Depiro, Albert Cernadas, Nunzio Lagrasso, Richard Dehmer, Edward Aulisi, Vincent Aulisi, Thomas Leonardis, Robert Ruiz, Michael Trueba, Ramiro Quintans, Salvatore Lagrasso, Anthony Alfano, Tonino Colantonio, John Hartmann, Giuseppe Pugliese, First Superseding Indictment, 1-10-2011

[106] https://www.courtlistener.com/opinion/2128988/united-states-v-international-longshoremens-assn/

enterprise that is comprised of the members of the Gambino and Genovese families operating on the Waterfront and their associates and co-conspirators in the ILA and other legitimate Waterfront organisations.

📁 American Stevedoring, Inc. v. ILA et al.[107]

In 2013, American Stevedoring Inc. filed a civil RICO lawsuit accusing the International Longshoremen's Association, the ILA's president and several others of forcing the company to sell its operations at the Port of New York and New Jersey. The case was before the court for two years. In 2015 the parties agreed and executed a settlement agreement after they went into mediation[108]. We can still look at the claim as an example of conduct among big players in the port environment.

The defendants are presented together as an enterprise, including the ILA, the executive members of the ILA, the individual members of the ILA local unions ("Locals") and other

---

[107] American Stevedoring, Inc., Plaintiff V. – International Longshoremen's Association, Afl-Cio, Harold J. Daggett (President), Stephen Knott (General Vice President), Louis Pernice (Vice President), Nysa-Ila Pension Fund: Joseph Curt (Co-Chairman), Port Police and Guards Union (PPGU), John T. Oates (President), Paul Punturieri (Vice President), NYSA-PPGU Pension Fund, Michael Farrino, and Joseph Pollio, Defendants, Case 1:13-cv-00918-UA, United States District Court Southern District Of New York
[108] https://www.courtlistener.com/recap/gov.uscourts.nysd.407617.105.0.pdf

ILA subordinate labor organisations, the trustees of the New York Shipping Association (NYSA)-ILA Pension Trust Fund, the Port Police and Guards Union (PPGU), the executive members of the PPGU, the individual members of PPGU Locals and other PPGU subordinate labor organisations, the trustees of the NYSA-PPGU Fund and a few other individuals. The dispute related to American's reluctant agreement in 2011 to sell its operations at the Red Hook terminal in Brooklyn and at Port Newark. American's operations were sold in September 2011 to Red Hook Container Terminal LLC. American claimed the ILA wanted to oust the company because it was unwilling to participate in *"illegal and corrupt activities"* including no-show jobs, loan-sharking and bogus insurance claims.

American claims that the defendants acted in a pattern of racketeering activities including, among other things, the establishment of a syndicate linked to organized crime (the "Waterfront Group"). This case is ultimately about recovery of damages as a result of a particular scheme directed at American by the Waterfront Group, to oust American from its business conducted at the New York and New Jersey Ports. However, the claimant also affirms that the Waterfront Group had first attempted to coerce American to participate in racketeering activities, and then eventually retaliated against American when American refused to do so. The claim proceeds by listing and connecting all the dots among the individuals and structures of the Waterfront Group, their indictments or convictions for crimes and their association with organised crime and illicit activities, including illegal gambling, loan sharking, extortion, labour racketeering, witness retaliation, mail fraud, wire fraud etc[109].

One of the main arguments in this claim is that notwithstanding the many convictions and investigations, and despite evidence of association with organised crime and racketeering activity, various high-ranking members of the ILA have been re-elected. In particular, American's claim focused on the chief role of the President of the ILA, Harold Daggett in the scheme of the extortion and particularly in the pressure on American to sign an agreement with the Port Authority, by which American would be ejected from the Terminals, with control to be taken over by Red Hook Container Terminal LLC, a company favored by the Waterfront Group over American. Using the mechanism of a port-wide strike, the ILA planned to coerce the signature of the agreement and eventually succeeded.

III. The difficulty of investigating and curbing corruption within and around the Port Authority.

The Port Authority of New York and New Jersey (PANYNJ) is a joint venture between the U.S. states of New York and New Jersey, established in 1921 to take care, initially of port commerce. Today the mandate of the Port Authority is considerably larger as it oversees much of the regional transportation infrastructure, including bridges, tunnels,

---

[109] Exhibit 2 of the claim -
https://www.courtlistener.com/recap/gov.uscourts.nysd.407617.1.2.pdf

airports, and seaports, within the geographical jurisdiction of the Port of New York and New Jersey. The Port Authority is headquartered at the World Trade Center and is a member of the Real Estate Board of New York. At the port, the authority operates from Port Newark–Elizabeth Marine Terminal. The agency has its own 1,700-member Port Authority Police Department.

On first glance to the media of the last years, it is quite obvious that the Port Authority has been connected to a number of scandals related to several key players, 'power brokers', in the political arena of New York and New Jersey. Some of these scandals stemmed from within the Authority, some others affected the functioning of the Authority. For example, in July 2016, the former chairman of the Port Authority of New York and New Jersey, **David Samson**, pleaded guilty in a probe examining whether he used his office for personal gain. He was under investigation for nearly three years by federal prosecutors for trading official actions for the resumption of a direct flight by United Airlines from Newark Airport to Columbia airport, near his country home in South Carolina[110].

In 2018 a multimillion-dollar scandal related to the acquisition of government contracts through bribery and collusion[111]. Overall, 13 individuals and 9 companies were charged for engaging in three separate schemes involving

---

[110] US v. David Samson, Case 2:16-cr-00334-JLL Document 1 Filed 07/14/16

[111] https://www1.nyc.gov/assets/doi/reports/pdf/2018/April/ContractingReport41718_final2.pdf

bribery, business fraud, and political campaign contributions. For construction management companies, public works are highly-prized jobs, and any competitive edge in the bidding process could mean the difference in the award of a contract worth millions. The corrupted process involved several leading construction management companies and executives, and a mid-level government employee (**Mr Ifeanyi Madu**) whose leaks to the companies enabled hundreds of millions of dollars in fraud. Mr Madu, an employee with the New York City Department of Environmental Protection (DEP), would offer confidential selection committee info, advance scopes of work, score sheets and cost estimates, in exchange for various benefits, including Broadway tickets, hotel stays, fine dining and millions of subcontracts for his companies. The case was handled by the Manhattan DA Construction Fraud Task Force in partnership with the Port Authority Inspector General's Office.

As construction is an evergreen industry for organised crime in NYC, other influences and attempts of collusion and corruption involving the Port Authority don't surprise. For example, in April 2017, **Vincent Vertuccio**[112], who has maintained a long affiliation with the Bonanno organised crime family of La Cosa Nostra, pleaded guilty at the federal courthouse in Brooklyn, New York, to conspiring to alter records for use in a grand jury investigation and to making and subscribing a false tax return. Vertuccio was under investigation

---

[112] https://www.justice.gov/usao-edny/pr/secret-partner-one-world-trade-center-construction-firm-pleads-guilty-obstruction

by a grand jury in the Eastern District of New York for conspiring to defraud the Port Authority of New York and New Jersey in connection with the One World Trade Center project located in lower Manhattan, as well as related money laundering and tax crimes. Vertuccio had hidden his control of Crimson Construction Corporation (Crimson) during the bidding process for the One World Trade Center project in light of his ties to organized crime and so as to hide taxable income that he received through Crimson.

In 1992 **the Port Authority of NY & NJ's Office of Inspector General (OIG)** was set up to keep the agency corruption-free. The OIG detects, receives, and investigates allegations of fraud, corruption, and abuse with respect to employees, or other individuals or organisations doing business with the Port Authority. The OIG has attempted a number of strategies to curb corruption in the past decades, and many of these strategies are aimed at low level corruption, thus outside of the direct scope of this project. These strategies are prevention-oriented models including background checks of individuals and businesses to ensure integrity and also confirm that no-one with links with organised crime is engaging with the port authority. These integrity monitoring activities include vetting of contractors and subcontractors. This also includes companies working at the port, including those who get permits or leases from the terminal companies for renovation works or short-term engagements.

The OIG confirms the general impression of other institutions that the type of corruption that organised crime families engages in nowadays is individual and not systemic anymore. Rather than corruption a whole industry (for example, construction), a single individual or a company might be targeted for unduly influence by organised crime. It is unclear whether this is a case of evidence by absence or absence by evidence once more, considering some reflections shared by the NYPD on the pervasive nature of NYC crime families in traditional businesses and unions, including those in the construction sector.

Research notes and emerging themes

The following themes have emerged from research fieldwork and notes as deserving of further attention and scrutiny, in no particular order:

A. In terms of trafficking, it is impressive to note the efforts that the USA put into **outbound** controls from abroad, through the Container Security Initiative. It is unclear, however, whether the same degree of care is exercised from within, as controls over outbound containers are essentially, like in other countries, an exception rather than a rule.
B. It is maintained by media and other public sources, that the US is one of the main producers of **electronic waste**.

According to UNODC[113], in the United States, the analysis of prosecutions for the illegal export certain types of e-waste has revealed that the culprits are seemingly **legitimate recycling firms.** Usually, recycling firms tasked with disposing of e-waste in accordance with US law have to charge their clients for recycling fees. Some companies would sell the e-waste to brokers representing foreign buyers and shipped the waste to other countries, i.e. China, instead. The e-waste buyers in the East Asia and Pacific region are usually brokers and waste traders. Verifiable information on links between e-waste trafficking and other forms of transnational organised crimes is scarce, and it has not been discussed by any of the participants.

C. Much of what happens around the Port of New York/New Jersey – in a similar fashion to other states – is about **political and public management of the city** of New York and the relationships among the elites also in the state of New Jersey. In particular the relevance of the port businesses can be seen impacting the following:
  a. The **survival of the Waterfront Commission**[114], attacked by different political factions, as well as

---

[113] https://www.unodc.org/documents/toc/Reports/TOCTA-EA-Pacific/TOCTA_EAP_c09.pdf

[114] https://www.politico.com/states/new-york/albany/story/2019/05/29/judge-strikes-down-law-that-sought-to-abolish-waterfront-commission-1033593 and
https://www.politico.com/states/new-

by high-ranking members of the ILA, and the NYSA. While for now plans to dismiss the agency seem under control, both ILA, NYSA and political supporters of this plan say the agency has become an impediment to economic growth.
b. The **recruitment process of workforce at the port** has become a nodal issue as well. While the Waterfront Commission detains powers of scrutiny over new hires, the ILA is the one that proposes new hires and generally handles recruitment. The Commission's involvement in the hiring process for dock workers is seen unfavourably by both the ILA and the NYSA as it slows down processes and it interferes with business and contracts. **Current trends in recruitment** to understand the actual percentage of organised crime infiltration or attempt of infiltration that the Waterfront Commission detects in their checks needs to be monitored, and possibly strengthened, as it does not seem to have slowed down.
c. The existence of big players in the local and bi-state battles around the Commission, the trade unions' networks, the Port Authority's voice and more generally, the **networks of power**

---

york/albany/story/2020/02/14/lesniak-could-face-calls-for-recusal-if-named-to-waterfront-commission-1261567 surrounding the interests on the waterfront are concerning. That the Civil RICO case against the ILA has been pending since 2007 is one of the examples given of the difficulty to disentangle these networks of powers. Similarly, different conflict of interests – for example of politicians who also serve on the board of the NYSA or ILA high ranking members who donate to political parties who, in turn, support the ILA, also give reasons for concern. More generally, slowing down legal proceedings and abusing powers to impede progress on regulations and controls seem to be the used tactics.

D. The role of the **unions** in the port and those dealing with the Port Authority (there are 22 unions normally engaging with the Port Authority) is extensive and as such is prone to being used and abused to reach positions of privilege and of mutual, particularistic, benefit. Even though links with organised crime and the unions have been largely curbed in the last decades, influence on essential and key positions is still not only possible but very likely.

E. (Illegally) controlling a large industry is at times only a matter of controlling an essential service of that industry, by, for example, extracting monopoly profit. In the port of NY/NJ, control over the workforce, slowing it down or speeding it up, its contracts and conditions, has been considered historically a way to control the port. Even though practices have evolved and the economy of the waterfront is now more complex than in previous years, this 'mentality' has been flagged as still enduring. Even in the complexity of the port economy, however, **there are very few moving parts in the port economy** – parts that do not depend from one another – in the port. While the trades are indeed global, the relationships and the workforce remain a local business and as such can be object and subject of abuse.

Case Study 5
Liverpool, UK

Photo: Seaforth, January 2020, Author's rights

General information

The Port of Liverpool sits on both banks of the River Mersey in a strategic point within the North West of the United Kingdom. The Port is 12.1 km long (7.5 miles) of dock system that runs from Brunswick Dock in Liverpool to Seaforth Dock, Seaforth, on the east side of the River Mersey and the Birkenhead Docks between Birkenhead and Wallasey on the west side of the river. The port runs through the **River Mersey** eastwards to and excluding Garston docks (in the city) and the Manchester Ship Canal; it includes, therefore, Seaforth, Bromborough & Tranmere. The port was extended in 2016 by the building of an in-river terminal at Seaforth Dock, name Liverpool2. The terminal, a £400m deep-water container terminal, can berth two 14,000 container Post-Panamax ships. This has doubled the container capacity of the port and made Liverpool one of the country's best-equipped and connected terminals. In 2017, Liverpool was the UK's fourth largest port by tonnage of freight, handling 32.5 million tonnes[115], and this remained unchanged in 2018[116]- In 2018 as well, 6.7 thousand cargo vessels arrived in Liverpool in comparison to Dover which scores first in these statistics with 17.7 thousand. Mainly

---

[115]https://assets.publishing.service.gov.uk/government/uploads/system/uploads/attachment_data/file/762200/port-freight-statistics-2017.pdf
[116]https://assets.publishing.service.gov.uk/government/uploads/system/uploads/attachment_data/file/826446/port-freight-statistics-2018.pdf

handling crude oil, RoRo, containers, agricultural products, oil products, coal, other dry bulk, ores, passengers, a total of 820 thousand TEU were mobilised in Liverpool in both directions (415 thousand TEU outward and 403 thousand TEU inward traffic)[117]. Among the countries for inward trafficking into Liverpool are majorly the rest of the EU (which accounts for over 40% of traffic), then USA, Canada, Argentina, Brazil[118]. The Port of Liverpool was a *free port* between 1984 and 2012.

Port ownership in the UK falls into three categories: privately owned ports; trust ports; and municipal ports owned by local government authorities. Liverpool originally a trust port, but in 1971 in order to avoid bankruptcy the Mersey Docks and Harbour Board was corporatized as the Mersey Docks and Harbour Company (a mixed public-private sector company). In 2005 the port was privatised and acquired by Peel Holdings. Many of the privatised ports have since changed hands again and now there are a handful of major port groups operating across the UK. **Peel Ports Group** now owns Liverpool1 and Liverpool2, the whole port of Liverpool and also employs the Port Police.

---

[117] UK major port freight traffic, by port and year (filter by direction and cargo type), from 2000 - https://www.gov.uk/government/statistical-data-sets/port-and-domestic-waterborne-freight-statistics-port#all-port-traffic-totals-major-and-minor

[118] UK major port traffic, port level downloadable dataset: 2000 – 2018 - https://www.gov.uk/government/statistical-data-sets/port-and-domestic-waterborne-freight-statistics-port#all-port-traffic-totals-major-and-minor

Policing and Security Authorities

Probably due to the different governance setting of the ports in UK and Liverpool as well, the amount of available data to collect during the course of the project was inferior to other ports. A total of 8 meetings were held, in the form of collective interviews or individual interviews with: Merseyside Police – Organised Crime Unit, North Western Regional Organised Crime Unit, Security at Port of Liverpool (Seaforth), Port Police Liverpool (Peel Group), National Crime Agency – Intelligence Command, National Crime Agency – Drug Threat Assessment, Border Force Intelligence Command (Merseyside), Associated British Ports – Security.

Illicit Trafficking

Drug Trafficking

National and international authorities have identified routes and mobility mechanisms of drug shipments involving Liverpool port or Liverpool-based criminal networks over a much larger area than just Merseyside. Let's consider some of the cases and events reported at the national and international levels.

📁 In March 2020, the National Crime Agency (NCA) reported[119] that one of the **"most wanted" fugitives** in the UK – had been arrested in Operation Captura, which targets fugitives suspected to be hiding out among the UK national community in parts of Spain. The man, from Liverpool, is the alleged head of a cocaine trafficking group through Merseyside. On the most wanted list, there are other three men wanted for drug offences who are from Liverpool; their activities range from transportation and distribution of amphetamines in Scotland[120], to cocaine importation together with Dutch groups[121].

📁 In **December 2019** the NCA reported[122] on the arrest of a man from Liverpool in the Netherlands, thanks to a European Arrest Warrant after 5 years on the run. The man is the alleged ringleader of an organised criminal network, thought to be behind the importation of firearms through corrupt truck drivers from the

---

[119] https://www.nationalcrimeagency.gov.uk/news/merseyside-drug-trafficking-suspect-arrested-after-six-years-on-the-run?highlight=WyJtZXJzZXlzaWRlIl0=
[120] https://www.nationalcrimeagency.gov.uk/most-wanted/mark-quinn
[121] https://www.nationalcrimeagency.gov.uk/most-wanted/michael-paul-moogan
[122] https://www.nationalcrimeagency.gov.uk/news/one-of-the-uk-s-most-wanted-men-arrested-on-christmas-day-in-the-netherlands?highlight=WyJsaXZlcnBvb2wiLCJsaXZlcnBvb2wncyJd

Netherlands into the UK and also wanted for drug offences (conspiracy to supply class A and B drugs) by Merseyside Police.

📁 In **August 2019** Border Force seized more than 250 kilograms of cocaine, after an investigation led to the interception of a yacht off the coast of Wales (escorting it to Fishguard port). NCA intelligence after cooperation with Spanish national police[123] had identified the vessel, the Sy Atrevido, as carrying a large drugs shipment to the UK from South America. Around 750kgs of cocaine were found with a wholesale value of around £24 million and a potential street value of £60 million once cut. The operation led to the arrest of two people from Liverpool on board of the yacht and four others arrested later in Liverpool and Loughborough. It is believed the drugs were destined to the Merseyside area and they were coming from a seller in Mallorca, Spain[124].

📁 A case collected in **Genova** reported of a seizure of 100 kgs of cocaine seized by Customs for the Direzione Distettuale Antimafia in Genova, at the terminal Genova

---

[123] https://www.nationalcrimeagency.gov.uk/news/huge-cocaine-haul-recovered-from-yacht-in-wales?highlight=WyJsaXZlcnBvb2wiLCJsaXZlcnBvb2wncyJd
[124] https://www.nationalcrimeagency.gov.uk/news/drug-smuggling-duo-from-liverpool-who-sailed-huge-haul-of-cocaine-across-the-atlantic-jailed-for-33-years?highlight=WyJsaXZlcnBvb2wiLCJsaXZlcnBvb2wncyJd

Pra' – Voltri (VTE) **in June 2019**. The narcotics was found in a container transporting refrigerated transporting frozen fish - on the MSC Nuria – a ship built in 2008 and registered with the Panama maritime registry. MSC Nuria's destination was scheduled for June 18th and it was the Port of Liverpool; the ship was coming from Montreal, Canada, from where it had left on June 10th. The frozen fish appeared to be destined to a commercial company in Milan, but it was unclear where the two hidde of cocaine were supposed to be offloaded and whether they were also destined to Milan.

In **June 2018** 400kgs of cannabis[125], worth 4 million pounds, were seized at the Port of Liverpool and led to the arrest of seven men found on board of the ship. Border Force and NCA found the drug concealed in crates of lettuce on board the vessel Wec Vermeer arrived from Spain. The authorities kept the container under covert surveillance for three days to follow the importation and eventually made their arrest after following the container to industrial premises in Lancashire.

In **July 2017**, an investigation by The Times[126] reported on an NCA-led investigation on a Romanian-based

---

[125] https://www.telegraph.co.uk/news/2018/06/01/police-smash-plot-smuggle-4m-worth-cannabis-uk/
[126] https://www.thetimes.co.uk/article/brutal-mexican-cartel-forms-pact-to-flood-uk-with-drugs-8wln52lb8

network that supported the Mexican Sinaloa Cartel (headed by convicted Joaquin Guzman, known as 'El Chapo') in bringing drugs into the UK, thanks to their capability to drive HGVs (Heavy Goods Vehicles) to import large amounts of cocaine into the UK on a weekly basis[127]. Through places such as Liverpool's docks and ports in Dover, Felixstowe and Harwich drugs transit to the UK from other European entry points (such as airports or ports in Belgium or Germany or the Netherlands or Spain). The investigation followed intelligence of NCA tracked UK-based criminals who had travelled to or established themselves in Mexico to facilitate the supply and transportation of drugs.

In 2015, the **Irish Court of Appeal**[128] heard a case related to facts in 2008, when three people, sailing the yacht 'Dances with Waves' outside of Irish territorial waters were found carrying cocaine weighing 1,504 kg. and valued at between €100 and €400 million. The suspect vessel was identified as a result of confidential information supplied to the Irish Joint Taskforce on Drugs ("JTF") by the Maritime Analysis and Operations Centre for Narcotics (MAOCN) in Lisbon, Portugal. The three men were charged for using a ship for drug trafficking

---

[127] https://www.occrp.org/en/daily/6765-uk-el-chapo-s-cartel-joins-forces-with-romanian-gangsters-to-smuggle-cocaine
[128] Director of Public Prosecutions -v- Wiggins [2015] IECA 178 (31 July 2015) URL: http://www.bailii.org/ie/cases/IECA/2015/CA178.html

and subsequently confessed and were detained. The vessel had been registered in Liverpool.

There are three emerging issues on data collection for the port of Liverpool:

1. The port has a reputation as a drug hub but there are no clear figures available on how many seizures and/or drug importation are estimated through Liverpool docks, in the same way as there is **no data** on other ports.
2. **News** – and also some cases collected for the other ports – mention Liverpool as the destination port or a middle point of arrival for the narcotics (seized elsewhere), but it is difficult to confirm some of these cases with other open data.
3. National authorities – especially those based in London – confirm that **criminality from Liverpool echoes** over drug importations across the country.

In connection to point one, it is worth remembering the statements from a **European Parliament's thematic report** in 2012 that was looking at drug cartels' links with criminal groups in Europe[129]. It must be reminded as well that **up until**

---

[129] Special Committee on Organised Crime, Corruption and Money Laundering (CRIM) 2012-2013 - Thematic Paper on Organised Crime - Drug Cartels and their Links with European Organised Crime

2012 Liverpool was a free port. The report confirms that **Mexico's drug cartels** may have found a new route through the English port city of Liverpool for smuggling cocaine into Britain and the rest of Europe, working closely with local gangs to distribute the drug. According to the report, Liverpool port had become a hib for cocaine smuggling and a valid alternative to smuggling routes through West Africa and through Spain. In this new partnerships, criminal groups in Merseyside act to arrange transport to other key places in the UK.

In connection to the third point, in a report on county lines intelligence in the UK[130], the NCA has confirmed that the greatest number of **county lines** in the country continue to originate from the area covered by the Metropolitan Police Service – London - (approximately 15% of individual deal lines), followed by the West Midlands Police (9%) and Merseyside Police (7%) force areas. This confirms that groups from Merseyside and the nearby West Midlands areas have a **disproportionate weight** over drug trade nationally[131].

September 2012
https://www.europarl.europa.eu/cmsdata/175904/20121016ATT53710EN.pdf, page 4

[130] https://www.nationalcrimeagency.gov.uk/who-we-are/publications/257-county-lines-drug-supply-vulnerability-and-harm-2018/file

[131] https://www.academia.edu/1222407/Mersey_heat_-_Gang_culture_in_Liverpool

What else can we learn from/about illicit trafficking and trade in Liverpool?

I. There is a threshold of tolerability about what is supposedly going on around the port, through the port, of Liverpool. Investigations on internal threats are risk-based, intelligence-based and discoveries are also random. Huge quantities of **cocaine** continue to be found – outside the port and around or in the city – but the price of cocaine has not gone up, which indicates that the market is saturated.

II. Trends are confirmed also in Liverpool, regarding **stolen vehicles** across Merseyside and the Manchester area shipped out to western African routes through Liverpool port. There is suspicion related to a company arranging the outgoing containers and involved in this business across the whole of the UK.

III. **Counterfeit goods** do constitute a concern because of the amount of money they involve, especially when goods are sold at the street level. These goods are necessarily coming through containers but it is difficult to track them before arrival. There seems to be a **diversification** of activities across criminal groups so that groups that previously were involved in drugs, or tobacco smuggling, are now engaged in contraband and counterfeit as it is less risky.

IV. The approach to detection and investigation remains more national than locally focused on Liverpool. There are differences in border threats at the North and the South of the countries, for illicit trade; in the North, including Liverpool, the focus remains on goods, in the South it is more on people and this affects resourcing. In Liverpool, in addition to cross-continent movements of containers, the trade with Ireland is a concern for Border Force.

V. In terms of **security**, it seems more likely that contraband or drugs are coming to Liverpool docks through hijacking of **legitimate companies' legal routes of trade,** rather than rip-on/rip-off that is instead displaced and would stand out on the premises of the port. **Financial registration data** collected for commercial intelligence can be used for security checks as well, but following up on what appear to be money laundering activities or other forms of economic crimes and frauds (through companies) is difficult to follow up with HMRC or other relevant authorities.

VI. It is unconceivable for law enforcement that the type of criminality in and around Liverpool does not reach out to the port or port workers, who move different commodities, including illicit ones, and might benefit from one off payment if they are willing and capable. There is a perception, by local authorities, that **Merseyside is still largely untouchable**; if a gang from Manchester appears into Liverpool to buy stolen cars, a feud is likely to erupt. This is likely to have echo over the port as well.

VII. **Local investigators**, in Liverpool city and in Merseyside region, agree that a large part of Merseyside criminality stems from the port; first because of new business opportunities that will increase direct routes from North America, and second because of the importance of the trafficking networks through Merseyside for which criminality at the port was for a long time a badge of honour.

VIII. **International investigations**, especially in large European ports (i.e. Antwerp and Rotterdam) confirm that in many cases intercepted shipments were directed to the UK, thus also confirming that there are **less direct routes of illicit trades to the UK** and Liverpool than there are indirect ones. Whenever a shipment is intercepted outside of the UK, national law enforcement in Liverpool expects some backlashes in the city.

IX. Available intelligence on current illicit trades, especially drugs, does not provide much insight on the connection between traffickers and importers from and through Liverpool. The networks appear completely diffused. Intelligence actually shows that **importers** are often **outside of the UK,** in jurisdictions that might be difficult to reach, i.e. Thailand or other Asian countries, and with expat communities that protect them. Often, there are suspicions about corrupted officials in foreign ports that support some of the trafficking networks of these individuals into the UK, including Liverpool.

Infiltration in the legal economy, corruption and governance issues

There was no indication of any case of corruption nor illicit governance as the ones described for the other ports in this report. The issues with governance at the port of Liverpool, with some sort of echo for security and policing of organised crime are related – to a minor extent - to the reputation of the owners and the companies at the port on one side and – to a larger extent – to the post-Brexit scenario and the proposal to establish 10 free ports in the UK, including Liverpool, since 2021.

Peel Port and port economics

The complexity of the **private governance** in Liverpool, de facto in the hands of **Peel Group**, has raised a number of questions related to the power and accountability linked to a conglomerate that has hundreds of subsidiaries and increasing economic power over the region[132]. The problem with

---

[132] ExUrbe, 2013, "Peel and the Liverpool City Region: Predatory Capitalism or Providential Corporatism."

overlapping public and private interests also poses questions around transparency[133]. An infrastructure, transport and real estate investment group, Peel owns holdings in land and property, transport (including ports and airports), logistics, retail, energy and media (MediaCityUK, home of the BBC in Salford). ExUrbe, a think-thank that operated in Liverpool in 2013 called for more scrutiny over Peel Group around the following aspects[134]:

- its financial arrangements;
- the extent and complexity of its corporate structure;
- its experience and 'track record' on delivering major development projects;
- the credibility of the evidence it produces in-house or via paid consultants to support its causes;
- the power of its PR machine.

Called one of the most secretive companies in the UK[135], Peel Group obviously faces some of the vicissitudes of all big corporations, including increased public scrutiny[136]. It particular,

---

http://media.wix.com/ugd/440822_22c65849313bcedd42dc15d57426cd04.pdf

[133] https://www.opendemocracy.net/en/opendemocracyuk/peel-power-real-northern-powerhouse/

[134] ExUrbe., page 213

[135] https://www.theguardian.com/environment/2019/apr/19/who-owns-england-secretive-companies-hoarding-land

[136] https://www.manchestereveningnews.co.uk/news/greater-manchester-news/property-giant-peel-group-accused-4290988

Peel has attracted criticism for using the Isle of Man, a low-tax jurisdiction, as its base for the holding company[137], but the accusation has not led to anything concrete, if not a stronger statement by the group over the commitment to not engage in any contract that might lead to avoidance of taxes[138].

In November 2019[139], Peel Ports agreed a 15-year contract extension with ACL (Atlantic Container Line) on container and ro-ro operations at the Port of Liverpool, until 2035, marking ACL's confidence in the growing volume of transatlantic trade between the UK and North America. ACL is part of the **Grimaldi Group company**, the largest ocean carrier operating at Liverpool's Royal Seaforth Container Terminal and the port's longest serving container carrier. The ACL transmits more than 125,000 units of containers, cars and RoRo machinery annually, and supports a supply chain with a critical link between the UK's export and import trades. In a case collected for the Italian side of this project, Grimaldi Group appeared as the sole beneficiary in a court case[140] of abuse of office and fraudulent activity involving the Authority of the **Port of Livorno** (Italy) and three companies operating in the port of Livorno that were all favoring

---

[137] https://www.ft.com/content/497be3f0-da7f-11e7-a039-c64b1c09b482
[138] https://www.peel.co.uk/wp-content/uploads/2019/07/Peel-Group-tax-strategy-2019.pdf
[139] http://www.ship2shore.it/en/shipping/grimaldi-renovates-its-loyalty-to-liverpool_72344.htm
[140] Giudice per l'Udienza Preliminare presso il Tribunale di Livorno, Sentenza di Rinvio a Giudizio, N. 1391/19 R.G.N.R.

the affairs of Grimaldi in violation of the laws of competition and fair trade. In that occasion, the public prosecutor argued that there was an ongoing criminal conduct, which tended to favour Grimaldi in their management of port contracts as they were (are) the most relevant economic and strategic power in the port. Within this conduct of diffused **trafficking of favours,** other companies in Livorno had been affected. Even though in that case there is no evidence of misconduct from Grimaldi Group, this case is particularly interesting because it suggested – albeit in a different location – that when private and public interests are handled within private rationales, the logic of favour tends to become the main one. This logic tends to serve the interests of single companies but it is not beneficial for the common good. This needs to be specifically addressed also in Liverpool, where **private interests are high** and also in light of the post-Brexit changes.

Freeports Post-Brexit

As said, Liverpool was a free port between 1984 and 2012. Proposals to set up 10 **free ports in the UK in the aftermath of Brexit**, and including Liverpool, has been on the table since 2018[141] and with a consultation open until April 2020[142]. There

---

[141] House of Commons, Debate Pack, Number CDP 2018-0211, 9 October 2018, The establishment of free ports in the UK available at https://commonslibrary.parliament.uk/research-briefings/cbp-8823/
[142] https://assets.publishing.service.gov.uk/government/uploads/system/uploads/attachment_data/file/864497/Freeports_Consultation.pdf

are not currently any free ports in the UK, though there is one on the Isle of Man. The Treasury currently has the power to designate free ports by Statutory Instrument under section 100A of the Customs and Excise Management Act (CEMA) 1979. Seven free ports operated in the UK at various points between 1984 and 2012. In July 2012, the Statutory Instruments that set up the remaining five free ports (Liverpool, Southampton, Port of Tilbury, Port of Sheerness and Prestwick Airport) expired.

A report published in 2018 by UK consultants Mace[143] said Liverpool alone could see the creation of up to 12,000 high-value jobs as a result of setting up freeport status. The report identified seven UK locations as being ideally placed to benefit – Liverpool, Immingham & Grimsby Ports, Hull Port, Rivers Hull & Humber, Tees & Hartlepool, Tyne and Manchester Airport. Representative body Mersey Maritime is backing the policy as is Port of Liverpool operator Peel Ports.

Obviously at the core of the new proposal to set up 10 free ports in the UK lies an economic motivation, to **boost the economy post-Brexit**. As part of the consultation, the government is seeking views on removing low tariffs, tariffs on key inputs to production and tariffs where the UK has zero or limited domestic production. Commentators have raised issues over the implications that freeports might have for security and criminality[144]. In particular, one of the problems would be in the

---

[143] https://www.macegroup.com/perspectives/180617-the-ultimate-boost-for-britains-economy
[144] https://shoc.rusi.org/informer/freeports-harbouring-criminality-brexit-britain

lack of obligation for freeport administrators to report suspicious transactions to authorities; despite the attempts to increase regulations[145], they exit from the EU still leaves way to grey zones. A March 2019 report by the European Parliament[146] notes that free zones, originally intended as spaces to store merchandise in transit, have become popular for the storage of substitute assets, including art, precious stones, antiques, gold and wine collections financed from unknown sources. Also, notes the EU parliament, free zones can have the same effects as **tax havens** as the motivations for their use include a high degree of secrecy and the deferral of import duties and indirect taxes. Additionally, *"money laundering risks in free ports are directly associated with money laundering risks in the substitute assets market"*, i.e. other cash/investment options including those that are harboured in warehouses at the ports as indicated above. In fact, by acting as **compensating chambers, warehouses** in between a no-tax zone and the rest of the country, they could allow for products to arrive and **'leak'** into

---

[145] The EU's fifth Anti-Money Laundering Directive (AMLD5) will classify freeports as 'non-financial obliged entities', requiring them to conduct the same customer due diligence expected of estate agents and notaries. However, firstly, this due diligence is only required for those trading in art and connected to transactions of €10,000 and above. Secondly, there is no obligation for freeport administrators to report suspicious transactions to their relevant national financial intelligence unit (see https://shoc.rusi.org/informer/freeports-harbouring-criminality-brexit-britain)

[146] https://www.europarl.europa.eu/cmsdata/162244/P8_TA-PROV(2019)0240.pdf section 4.2

the rest of the economy, and that includes illicit goods as well. Without customs checks, the true nature of the goods and their identity might easily be disguised. In this sense, free ports might actively disguise both goods and their owners' identity, thus fuelling the informal economy.

In 2018, the European Parliament had published another report[147] on the risks of tax evasion and money laundering associated to free ports, highlighting especially the risks for the art market and similar niche markets. Free ports resemble offshore financial centres; they offer both high security and discretion and allow transactions to be made without attracting the attention of regulators and direct tax authorities. As **tax fraud and tax evasion have been considered predicate offences for money laundering** since the entry into force of the Anti Money Laundering Directive IV in June 2017, the money laundering risks associated to the establishment of free ports is very high. It would be virtually impossible for a free port operator to establish whether a client did make the rightful declaration to the tax authorities in the country of tax residence before entering the port with certain goods.

147

https://www.europarl.europa.eu/cmsdata/155721/EPRS_STUD_627114_M oney%20laundering-FINAL.pdf

Research notes and emerging themes

The following themes have emerged from research fieldwork and notes as deserving of further attention and scrutiny, in no particular order:

A. Coordination remains a problem and trust issues among institutions have emerged. This could be one of the reasons for the lack of specific data for Liverpool. Additionally, even when law enforcement agencies **share data** not Peel port does not, as a private owner, which does create imbalances.

B. The business agenda of Liverpool seems to invest in the North-American and South American markets. The rationale is that much of the UK's container demand is closer to Liverpool than to the south-eastern ports of the UK. The question remains on **whether the ships will divert from the major trade lanes to serve Liverpool** rather than the current model whereby vessels traverse the shortest route to northwest Europe and the containers then must travel overland from southern UK ports to their destinations. This is also a **Brexit-related** question. According to authorities in Liverpool, post-Brexit will lead to greater volumes from shore-sea movements, as it will cost less to ship by sea from Spain, for example, than carry over produce in trucks within EU territory to the UK. Brexit might lead to **the increased use of containers**, as ferries will become more expensive to

use and more burdensome for checks on cargo on the customers' side.
C. In terms of **security regulations**, Brexit might not bring immediate risks, if not for the possibilities of stowaways hiding in containers from Europe into Liverpool. However, a grey area remains in the ability of port authorities to **detect corruption** on the docks, both for employees and for law enforcement agents accessing the ports.
D. Institutions often converge in linking the drug scene in Liverpool with the port, but the link remains unproved. The **city of Liverpool**, which has been home to many 'famous' UK drug traffickers (e.g. Curtis Warren) has shaped and still shapes the drug scene across the country. In particular, while it is taken as a given that the majority of drugs arrive into Liverpool, it is also considered that these drugs, especially **cocaine**, arrive into the country on containers to European ports and then to the southern English ports. Through lorries, boats, yachts, or other vehicles, they then make their way through Merseyside. There might be interests from individuals based in Liverpool and Merseyside to participate in this business but not through the port of Liverpool necessarily.
E. Networks based in the southern Coast of Spain show **connections to Merseyside**; in the same way authorities evidence a preponderance of people from Liverpool or Merseyside in drug trafficking cases outside of the UK.

F. The reason for such preponderance is linked to the drug scene in Liverpool, a **mafia-like underworld** where reputation and money reach out into all different areas of society, not just the purely illicit ones.

G. The **legacy** of individuals who have made the history of **drug trafficking** in Liverpool and the UK, of the likes of **Curtis Warren**, still endures and influences cocaine trade to the UK also today. The modus operandi of the group surrounding Warren remains an example to follow also today. Warren led an international network, even though he was based in Liverpool, acting in a diffused way throughout the country. Close to him, younger and senior individuals performed different tasks; some of them were very involved in social control techniques in Liverpool, by looking at car plates and hotel stays for example. Others were not based in Liverpool and were mostly operational in the drug trade business. The network was highly **dispersed**.

H. In Liverpool, **the city-port interface** for criminal ventures is particularly interesting and needs to be further investigated. This, specifically, in the light of the sophistication of some of the groups in the city that have long ago started investing in legal businesses, especially corruption. For example, since **operation Seahog** was launched in August 2006 to crackdown on illegitimate security firms in the construction industry, the knowledge of how underworld figures enter legitimate markets and industries has increased and does leave an open question on the business interests of organised crime in the city/infrastructure of Liverpool port.

Lessons Learned, Challenges & Recommendations

Illicit Trafficking

Across all port sites law enforcement's priority remains on investigating and disrupting drug trafficking through and in the port. Drug trafficking is considered a **high harm/high gain** kind of activity. On the one hand, potential harm to drug users is the reason why the stakes are high to disrupt drug importations. On the other hand, profits of the drug trade are bound to re-enter the economy, after being laundered, and can fuel further criminal activity in addition to affecting the legal economy.

Other forms of illicit trades are obviously recorded at all sites, especially **inbound**, with a specific emphasis on tobacco contraband; counterfeit goods (including pharmaceuticals); counterfeit food produce; counterfeit luxury goods and fashion. **Outbound** trafficking, especially waste, stolen vehicles, and cash, is also recorded. Due to, officially, a problem of resourcing but also in consideration of the **difficulty of measuring success** in this kind of endeavour, outbound trafficking is not a priority in any of the port sites. With the exception of the USA's Container Security Initiative (CSI) – which allows CBP and other US Agencies to request checks to outbound cargo abroad – border agencies and customs do no operate strategically in the controls and checks of outbound cargo from their waterfronts. Controls and checks are left to specific intelligence leads or, even more so, to randomness.

All groups involved in illicit drug trade in all port sites exhibit **hybrid ethnic compositions**. The ethnic connotation of organised crime is considered an unhelpful way to look at the city/port underworld. Location and specific ethnic connotations are not relevant for the groups involved in the trade, but they might be relevant for the origin of the product. Also, in all cities there is an understanding of how major players of the underworld are interested in drug importation to the city, with or without involving the port as a 'door'.

For other illicit trade, different from narcotics, there is a tendency for criminal groups to **specialise** in a specific trade. This specialisation can also be ethnic-driven. This is at times related to **cultural reasons** to specialisation (for example a certain type of contraband tobacco smuggled from Greece/Turkey to specifically serve the Greek/Turkish community). Other times, specialisation follows the specific characteristic, and **origin**, of a certain smuggled/counterfeit/illicit good (for example, counterfeit pharmaceuticals from China in the port of Melbourne, smuggled by predominantly Chinese groups).

Smuggling methods vary across sites, especially via cargo. There are, however, some trends that are worth pointing out across all sites:

* Overall *decrease of rip-on/rip-off* method for drug smuggling (probably due to increased difficulty in avoiding security mechanisms on site in ports, security displacement).
* Overall *increase of use of small vessels*, usually private boats (i.e. yachts) or other smaller vessels (including submarine). These can be mooring in smaller ports, as well as have the agility of faster travel in international waters. The trend is towards diffusion, dilution and fragmentation of drug importation 'jobs' as a reaction to security displacement of crime.
* Overall *increase of quantities smuggled* (as per detection) in containers, as containers are mostly meant to come out of the port.

Across all port sites, **investigation teams** work in partnerships with others: the port-city interface, for what concerns law enforcement, is very small on the waterfront. Security networks comprise terminal security, port authorities, port policing teams (whether federal, national or local); border force units, custom and excise representatives and so on. In order to disrupt terminals' business less – and also to allow for smarter allocation of resources - policing authorities rely more and more on **intelligence-based interventions** in the port, avoiding random and casual checks to container without prior knowledge on something to investigate on the cargo. The main challenge remains that these security networks often work with different security protocols, treating data according to various confidentiality levels and without disclosing it to one another, for legal reasons mainly. In particular, the role of **Border Agencies** in all port sites, is interesting: on one side, these institutions enjoy the highest degree of access into port terminals; on the other side, they are often hybrid institutions, in between a duty and excise agency and a law enforcement agency, which might lead to different prioritisation of daily work as well as different perceptions of their work and capability by others in the security network of the port.

🗀 RECOMMENDATIONS

I. **Security networks**, made up of all different authorities and institutions engaged in security and policing at a given port, should be established as permanent units meeting regularly and have shared data platforms.

II. A **tenant mentality** is often at play in the relationship between policing authorities and public institutions, and private owners of the port terminals (or in the case of Liverpool, the port territory). It is advised that security networks are 'chaired' periodically by a terminal employee alternating with a public body institution, to maintain balance.

III. These security network teams should include a **research & insight role** dedicated to the following themes (the list is not exhaustive) with specific reference to each port

and its conditions and peculiarities. This role should report monthly or bimonthly to the security network:
- *Cross-border issues updates:* these might include changes in drug production and supply mechanisms; changes in drug legislation around the world; changes in legislation pertaining waste in the country where the port exports the most; smuggling methods in trends around the world (diversified for region, for cargo and for type of shipment).
- *Debriefing and updates on criminality in the city* including, but not only, drug importation networks; corruption networks and investigations on power and crime.
- Debriefing and update on trade relationships in the port; this includes also a comparative look to other ports in the state/region of reference, as well as a cross-referencing of these with information from previous points.

IV. Identify ways to not solely rely on intelligence-based interventions, but using more random and casual checks to operate a **surprise effect on controls.** The predictability of crime prevention and suppression techniques works against policing intended purposes in the long run. This is specifically important, as we will see in the next section, to curb on the ability of individual employees or dock workers or border agents - victims or agents of corruption – to sell reliable information on the schedule of the port and the movement of authorities around shipments.

Corruption

Individual corruption is the most common door illicit networks use to complete their importations. Individual corruption is considered key to criminality on the waterfront, both as an enabler of illicit trades and as a stand-alone practice to acquire other types of benefits (including but not limited to money). In particular, illicit trade is often connected to occasional or systemic corruption of **dock workers**, indicated as the most common factor of persistent criminality on the waterfront. Individual corruption of port **employees**, terminal employees, police, custom, and border **agents**, is also considered a persistent feature of illicit trades in the port.

In this type of corruption, which could be more or less recurring/occasional, industrial relationships often play a role. Labour racketeering remains a high concern, together with other forms of **coercive systemic corruption** on the waterfront carried out by organised crime groups frequently and repeatedly *accessing* (and influencing) unions or other groups of workers.

In addition to individual circumstances of people engaging in corrupt behaviours (which might be related to money shortages or other needs), for illicit trades, it is the **function** of individuals that becomes crucial to **'access'**. Port employees, dock workers, custom, police, and border agents can help gain advantage of what matters in importations: getting a knowledge advantage (selling information about the port and the supply chain) and avoiding controls. This is linked to the peculiarity of the port economy, which remains obscure to many and has a very fragmented nature between global economic choices and local management.

Systemic forms of corruption, whether collusive or coercive, are often difficult to prove and detect. This is connected to the varied systems of investigating corruption at the border. A lot of emphasis is placed on individual corruption as enabler of other crimes (trafficking) and very thin are the boundaries between corrupt agents treated as offenders or as victims, when it comes to them providing doors or access keys to complete a 'job'. **Corruption** as **autonomous practice**, which, in ports, usually manifests as part of infiltration in the legal economy, is heavily **under-investigated** due to difficulty in considering the port space as a special environment deserving of ad-hoc procedures for anti-corruption. The split between policing units and law enforcement agencies investigating organised crime and institutions investigating corruption – with the sole exception of Italy and partially the United States – remains a concern when it comes to port sites.

🗁 RECOMMENDATIONS

I. Institution of a **port anti-corruption team** that both conducts their own investigations and receives investigation leads from organised crime units in the city and/or in the port. Similarly to the Waterfront Commission in New York, the port anti-corruption team should be independent from the port authority and from law enforcement but share data with both.

II. Adjust salary packages of dock workers, port employees, custom and border agents, on the basis of **ethics incentives** (including whistleblowing and other incremental benefits). Incentives should be based on the awareness of power relations in the industry and not offered as a bargain or as a form of trade.

III. The port anti-corruption team should be working as a **monitoring community**, for what concerns spotting different types of corruption (coercive or collusion-based).

IV. **Dispersion of discretionary power** should be considered in job allocation: no function should be left in solitary administration, to avoid exploitation; rotation of job rotas should be monitored by the port anti-corruption team.

Infiltration in the legal economy and governance issues

Infiltration in the port economy refers to attempts to influence or acquire business opportunities, ranging from infiltration in the supply chain to the provision of services on the grounds. Infiltration in the port economy emerges in all ports, albeit with different impact and different results. At the local level, **infiltration** of organised crime in the legal economy of the port manifests mostly as a **means to an end** – where the end is often **illicit trade**, to increase profit as well as laundering money. Employees or managers or other third-party brokers specialise in the port economy and can exploit this knowledge and sell it to the benefit of different criminal networks This manifests in two different scenarios.

- ✱ **Known companies** active in a variety of markets and businesses in the city (from food import-export to beauty salons, from furniture shops to car shops, from art dealers to phone companies) that normally use the maritime route for their supplies, are also occasionally or systematically used to disguise and conceal illicit products amongst their legitimate cargo. This can happen with or without awareness of the company managers. The knowledge a broker or an invested party needs in this scenario relates to:

- Warehousing/storage of container/cargo once arrived;
- Origin of cargo;
- Schedule of supplies;

★ **New companies** (including transport companies or import-export) are set up with the intent and purpose of creating means to access the port in semi-legitimate ways. In this case, knowledge needed relates to:
  - Access cards/security checks to be admitted on port premises;
  - Establishment of a credible supply route;
  - Avoidance of checks and alert of control;
  - Storage facilities/warehousing available.

The port economy is vulnerable to infiltration in terms of contracts for construction, security, logistics (including, warehousing) and transport, including large infrastructure (e.g. rails, roads). This is a form of **high-level infiltration**. These activities are mostly aimed at increasing profits; they are carried out by networks who are able to be active both through illegal and legal means, capable and willing to acquire economic power over certain economic sectors, whichever way. In the majority of port sites, investigators' knowledge of organised crime groups in the city includes the interests of some of these groups in the port. Brokers, businessmen, investors, legal professionals, financial consultants, and other third parties might engage in collusive behaviours forming cartels over tenders and engaging in unfair competition, through intimidation techniques or other forms of market exclusion. At times this can be done via corruption, at times it can be achieved through the use of other organised crime groups as enforcers. When this type of infiltration – usually associated to long-term, often large-scale contracts – becomes systemic this is a **problem of governance**.

The port economy is a rather small field albeit truly global, which still manifests and interacts with city-based powers (economic and political). Governance is, intuitively, informal among very few big players that all know each other (terminal operators, shipping lines, carriers). Attempts to distort this governance for criminal or deviant purposes, is, however, confined to the local level, especially when port management is closer to **political power**. This can happen when administrators/managers in the port authorities are Activities of infiltration and attempts to govern the port space vary depending on the nature, the level of sophistication and the amount of investment that organised crime groups have in the city. The port is a territory where influence, power and consensus are convergent with economic success in the city as in the port. The **port-city relationship** develops across a range of influential political and economic actors around the city, with the ability and the will to access the port administration to further their profit and increase their influence and power.

🗁 RECOMMENDATIONS

I. Efforts to police organised crime in ports needs to consider the whole **spectrum of sophistication** of organised crime groups, from those only engaged in profit-seeking activities, to those also or solely engaged in power-seeking ones (mafia-type). Any effort to curb organised crime on the waterfront needs a special units that look at **systemic corruption** as both enabling large-scale, recurring, trafficking, and as autonomous practice that distorts port governance.
II. Either through a special unit of research embedded in the port, or through a special anti-corruption unit as per abovementioned hypothesis, a specific outlook to infiltration is needed, as part of countering of organised crime in the port. These units have to have a **specific port-city relationship mandate** for organised crime and corruption. They ought to pair intelligence-led policing that is normally applied to cross-border trafficking investigation, to monitoring of public contracts and anti-collusion efforts.
III. Investigations in the **port-city relationship** need to depart from tracking the level of sophistication of certain groups and networks of power (among businesses men as much as professionals) and their willingness – in addition to their capability - to enter corruptive or collusive pacts with corporations or other business partners, or via small firms, to access resources (including contracts and administrative roles).

IV. Similarly, these investigations need to target the capability – in addition to the intent – of **key figures** (professionals, financial services, consultants) to bend and exploit legal loopholes for tenders, and access or allocation of funds and resources. Social networks analysis, of qualitative or quantitative type, could identify people in position of brokerage and influential figures in various markets and industries – those who could, essentially, sell information and knowledge of the system for others to exploit.

Intervening Factors

Brexit – Preliminary Forecast

Since the United Kingdom voted to leave the European Union in June 2016, and currently on the path to finally do so by end of December 2020, different scenarios on post-Brexit Britain have emerged. Some of these scenarios relate to borders, border security, and maritime trade. Readers are remanded to the Liverpool case study in this report for what concerns the proposals to introduce **freeports**, free trade zones, in ten ports in the UK. Since this project started in January 2019, and by the time it has ended in mid-2020, the proposal has been on the table and is very likely to gain traction. As it has been pointed out[148] the current UK proposal for freeports is not addressing a number of issues that relate to organised crime in ports. Indeed, freeports yield a number of criminal opportunities for illicit drug trade, counterfeit trade, money laundering, tax evasion and evasion of custom duties. In particular, the already existing **risk profiles** of a port are augmented by the existence of free trade zones due to[149]:

---

[148] RUSI Briefing Paper - Free Ports, Not Safe Havens Preventing Crime in the UK's Future Freeports - https://rusi.org/sites/default/files/27042020_freeports_final.pdf
[149] Ibid. pages 5-6

- Reduced customs controls compared to the rest of the country;
- Insufficient oversight of commercial activities in a freeport and inadequate record keeping;
- Prevalence of cash transactions and reduced anti-money laundering/counterterrorist financing (AML/CTF) oversight;
- Lack of reliable beneficial ownership records;
- Inadequate physical security due to the lack of clear freeport boundaries.

In addition to the freeport proposals, any formula, or deal, that will deliver Brexit poses a number of questions related to border security, trafficking, corruption and port governance in the UK and in relation to foreign partners, especially EU countries. Specific changes to the UK maritime regulations are on the way to be studied and assessed as it is still unclear, in mid 2020 what the legislative scenario will be[150].

---

[150] See: *The UK maritime sectors beyond Brexit*. A report on the impact of Brexit on UK shipping, maritime legal services, fisheries and trade by the Institute of Maritime Law and the Southampton Marine and Maritime Institute of the University of Southampton - https://eprints.soton.ac.uk/426985/1/Final_IML_Report_Brexit.pdf

The first concern is Maritime Security. A policy report by academics at the university of Bristol[151] has highlighted how the UK faces three critical challenges that Brexit will intensify: 1) A complex security environment with enormous transnational capacity (95% of all UK imports and ex-ports move by sea through over 400 British ports); 2) Current patchiness of capacity amongst different geographic spaces and regions; 3) The need to address problems of coordination across agencies delivering UK maritime security.

- ✴ In 2019, the UK government created the Joint Maritime Security Centre (JMSC) to coordinate all the different agencies involved and foster interaction between them, but it still very early to gauge any success.

When key **collective EU maritime governance arrangements** will either cease to apply or be revised, the UK might choose to regulate its own waters. This is the case of policies such as the Common Fisheries Policy[152], for which both UK and EU fishing boats had access to quotas in UK waters.

---

[151] Delivering UK maritime security after Brexit: time for a joined-up approach, by Professor Tim Edmunds (SPAIS, University of Bristol) and Dr Scott Edwards (SPAIS, University of Bristol), March 2020, http://www.bristol.ac.uk/media-library/sites/policybristol/briefings-and-reports-pdfs/SafeSeas%20report_v5.pdf

[152] Phillipson, J. and Symes, D. (2018) 'A sea of troubles': Brexit and the fisheries question, *Marine Policy*, Volume 90, Pages 168-173

- A sudden change of arrangements might bring to **loopholes** and grey areas to be exploited for criminal opportunities.

Indeed, illegal fishing, border violations, and disorders including blockades of ports, are all included in the scenario depicted by **Operation Yellowhammer**[153] that in August 2019 studied the worst-case planning assumption and impact of Brexit for the UK Government.

- Concurrent incidents will strain border agencies and institutions activating a response.

Amongst other things, Operation Yellowhammer also highlighted how the **Agri-food supply chain**, especially for fresh produce, could be severely impacted after Brexit; it is expected that availability and choice of produce will decrease and therefore prices for certain products might increase.

- This leaves a door open to **contraband** that in the food sector could be particularly lucrative between EU states and the UK.

Also, it might become troublesome for UK personnel to carry out inspections in other EU ports, including Ireland. According to Article 16(2) of Directive 2005/65/EC, the

---

[153]https://assets.publishing.service.gov.uk/government/uploads/system/uploads/attachment_data/file/831199/20190802_Latest_Yellowhammer_Planning_assumptions_CDL.pdf

personnel performing security inspections or handling confidential information (including the personnel of recognised security organisations) requires a **security vetting** of the Member State of which the person concerned is a national. This means that United Kingdom personnel (thus holding a security clearance from the United Kingdom) can no longer carry out the security inspections referred to in the Directive

> ✶ This could bring to decrease capacity of detection and increased **corruption risks.**

Other concerns relate to illicit trade and particularly drugs, in addition to the concerns related to freeports. **Cross-border crimes**, in the presence of uncertain times and policies or in the wake of changing protocols in border controls, are likely to increase For example, if cocaine production increases at the rate that it has increased in the past years (quadrupled in Colombia in the past four years) and the demand for cocaine in the UK is also increasing, cocaine trade to the UK will certainly not stop at Brexit.

> ✶ Cross-border drug supply is likely to continue or increase, and the ports will certainly be affected by this. The likelihood that the UK's borders will be an even more attractive destination for illicit goods, such as cocaine, especially after Brexit, is a realistic concern. This will also affect what is 'behind' the borders of ports; distribution networks for drugs and other illicit products will have to adapt to new regulations and changes in

supply networks; certain territories might become more attractive for criminal groups willing to invest in new opportunities.

It has been noted throughout this research that the majority of illicit drugs into Europe are routed through Spain, Netherlands and Belgium, key waypoints from South American ports, especially for cocaine. Heroin is mostly routed through the Balkans and mainland Europe. Increased controls at the borders in the UK, from EU countries might lead to two possible scenarios:

- ✸ Exploitation of **new routes** of trafficking that cut the risk of being checked at the borders repeatedly: this can involve either an increased use of smaller vessels (as seen, this is already a trend) and/or the abuse of new trade lines from Spain or from North America that, according to some ports (including Liverpool) will form after Brexit to secure the Atlantic routes.
- ✸ Should EU ports still be used for certain illicit trade routes, the results might be damaging for **public health**: with increased risks at the borders, it might be more expensive for traffickers to complete transactions in the short-medium term. This might bring to increase in drug prices until things settle down and adapt to the new normal and/or reduction in drug quality to keep supply affordable.

Lastly, a strategic assessment from the UK National Crime Agency (NCA)[154] warned that as UK businesses look to increase the amount of trade they have with non-EU countries after Brexit, the likelihood that they will be drawn into **corrupt practices** will increase.

* **Border corruption**, both in terms of administrative corruption and in terms of governance abuse, in the wake of a more complex regulatory system is likely to increase. In particular, with changing practices in port calls, an eye should be kept on port access and companies (UK and foreign) ownerships.
* The difficulty in curbing **corporate criminality** in the UK, as well as the increased challenges to run checks with European partners after Brexit, represent a concern in post-Brexit Britain, for what concerns corporate interests in ports.

Covid-19 Pandemic – Preliminary Forecast

Since January 2020, with peak in March 2020, almost all countries in the world have entered periods of lockdown in an attempt to boost protection from contagion by Coronavirus Covid-19. Lockdown measures have particularly hit European and Western world countries, by limiting people's movements

---

[154] https://www.nationalcrimeagency.gov.uk/who-we-are/publications/173-national-strategic-assessment-of-serious-and-organised-crime-2018/file

and slowing down – if not stopping completely – international business relations.

At the time of writing, May 2020, it is still hard to prognosticate future development both with the virus and with the economic impact of lockdowns and containment procedures. Ports play an essential role during a critical moment such as the pandemic, because food, cargoes, including those with life-saving supplies, cannot arrive to where they are needed if ports are not operational.

The Covid-19 pandemic has not modified neither the purposes nor the results of this research project. However, considerations can be advanced in relation to the future of port management with relation to organised crime and illicit, cross-border, trafficking through ports at this stage of the pandemic in light of studies and early observations about what has been happening in the port economy due to the pandemic[155]

> A. While there has been a steep reduction of trade in certain ports, at the end of April, the share of ports facing significant decreases in **container vessel calls** (in excess of a 25% drop) climbs to 11%, compared to less than 10% last week and only 2-3% in the first two weeks in which the Port Economics Impact Barometer survey run in early

---

[155] IAPH-WPSP Port Economic Impact Barometer
https://sustainableworldports.org/wp-content/uploads/WPSP-Port-Economic-Impact-Barometer-1-May-2020.pdf

April 2020. However, dockworkers, technical nautical services personnel, and the incidence of staff being placed on social wage schemes has been fluctuating during the pandemic.

B. **Port call procedure changes** (e.g. hygiene inspections, distancing of workforce, disruption of port or related services) have been reporting fewer delays in early May than in March. In particular, In April 2020 8 out of 10 ports did not impose any restrictions on container vessels with the same applying for 3 out of 4 ports for other cargo vessels.

C. Border checks, a lower availability of truck drivers and disruptions in terminal operations have negatively affected trucking operations in/out of the port area and to the hinterland during the pandemic and lockdowns. The end of April 2020 Port Economics Impact Barometer reports that about 18% of the ports report delays (6-24 hours) or heavy delays (> 24 hours) in cross- border **road transportation** with 2% of the ports indicating that cross-border trucking has been discontinued. This, however, is an improvement from March 2020, indicating that the situation is expected to go back to normal. Indeed, about two thirds of the ports witness normal operations in cross-border transport by truck and also by **rail**.

D. Interestingly, however, **trucks companies** appear as the most affected by the crisis, i.e. in some countries it was reported that more than 50% are actually closed; due to the present drop of the demand for services however, this has not affected services at ports.
E. **Warehousing and distribution** activities are improving in April/May 2020; they had seen a particularly difficult time, due to the complexity of mobility of people/workers. Partial or full lockdown measures in different countries can lead to the fall of demand for certain consumer products which leads to fall in warehousing and distribution activities. Hoarding behaviours, which seems to be improving in April and May, has also disrupted foodstuff supply chains. Ports were either under-utilising or over-utilising their storage facilities but currently the situation is going back to normal. Indeed, food products and medicines are the products that continue to be on the rise.

It seems obvious that the lasting impact of good flows may be minor due to the pandemic. It is clear that the deep **international integration of supply chains** and the resulting interdependencies are at the core of the economic disruption caused by the pandemic. Indeed, trends towards more **local value chains** have been recorded but it is hard to see the trend of international economic integration being reversed, especially if/when the pandemic crisis is contained. This is valid also for illicit international trade.

Focus should be kept on **Latin American countries** and the impact of Covid-19 pandemic and lockdown restriction on the **drug trade**. A lot will depend on the modes of transportation of the narcotics. Even with delays and stops to cargo travels, especially air transport, criminal networks can operate their businesses by changing routes, using unofficial border crossings and shifting trafficking modes, for example, instead of using commercial cargo by land, they might indeed increase available and informal maritime transportation using smaller vessels (i.e. fishing boats) or other allowed boats.

Drug trade

Cocaine
- On one side, seizures in European ports have revealed that **cocaine shipments** have been arriving in even larger quantities during the March-April 2020 period especially in Antwerp and Rotterdam. However, **cocaine production** appears to be only partially impeded in Colombia, as some producers are suffering from a shortage of gasoline. In Bolivia, Covid-19 is limiting the ability of state authorities to control coca bush cultivation, which could lead to an increase in coca

production. In Peru, however, a drop in the price of cocaine (over 45%) suggests a reduction in trafficking opportunities[156].

★ Even when containerised vessels have reduced calls in certain ports, the trend has been for some ocean carriers (like Maersk) to replace these cancellations by regional feeders with good frequency. As a result, the reduced number of long-haul calls has been counterbalanced[157].

★ As reported[158], Caribbean coast (Cartagena, Colombia), had a total throughput of 664,846 TEU during the first trimester in 2019, which increased 19% during the same period in 2020. The Pacific coast has experienced a decrease in its activity, since the port of Buenaventura, Colombia, experienced a drop of 11,3% in its activity during the first trimester in 2020 compared to the same period in 2019.

→ Cocaine shipments on the **Pacific route**, which is the main corridor of cocaine mobility (through

---

[156] Research Brief - COVID-19 and the drug supply chain: from production and trafficking to use - https://www.unodc.org/documents/data-and-analysis/covid/Covid-19-and-drug-supply-chain-Mai2020.pdf

[157] http://www.porteconomics.eu/2020/04/26/third-covid-19-world-ports-survey-report-the-impact-of-blank-sailings-starts-kicking-in/

[158] Sanchez, R. J. and Barleta, E. P. (2020). Latin American and Caribbean ports situation in
face of COVID-19, UN-ECLAC Report, 21 April 2020. Santiago Chile: UN-ECLAC. Available at http://www.porteconomics.eu/mdocs-posts/2020-latin-american-and-caribbean-ports-situation-in-face-of-covid-19-sanchez-and-barleta/?mdocs-cat=

Colombia and Ecuador travelling through Central America), appear more complicated as trade has decreased, but the same might not apply to the Caribbean routes.
→ The economic crisis that could follow the pandemic may lead more workers/farmers to increase or start engaging in coca cultivation in all the major cocaine-producing countries. The increase in coca leaves prices, as figures from Peru show, will increase competition among those producers who have easier access to traffickers and are 'higher up' in the supply chain.
→ As **demand** of cocaine is fluctuating (due to logistics of procurement and delays in arrival), price in the destination countries might increase too, to settle again to 'normal' prices as both supply and demand settle, once the pandemic restrictions are over. Overall reduction in cocaine **trafficking** in the near future, which might not last long though, can follow countries – like Peru – which are struggling with trafficking.
→ The **maritime trafficking** of cocaine, considering what we know about container movement is not impaired and it will easily pick up on current delays. Indeed, Latin American ports have not been heavily impacted, in terms of cargo

volumes, by the current crisis[159] and direct shipments of cocaine from Latin America to Europe can be arranged via smaller vessels (provided they don't attract too much attention if other vessels are not running).

Heroin
- ✱ As for **heroin**, the UN found indications of an increase in the use of maritime routes for trafficking heroin to Europe along the "southern route" (the Indian Ocean). This is also to avoid increased border controls on land from Mexico to the US or in Asia.
    - → This would indicate a change in the strategy of trafficking networks and an adaptation to COVID-19 measures, which might not last once these measures are lifted.
    - → Lower prices for heroin in some could be expected as trafficking via sea gets more difficult.

Synthetic drugs
- ✱ As for **meth and fentanyl** sales coming from the Mexican cartels are struggling because the coronavirus has closed borders and reduced supply chains from/in China, which are necessary for precursors drugs.

---
[159] Ibid

- ✶ Where precursor chemicals are supplied in the region or domestically, then production, and therefore trafficking, has not been impeded, if not only marginally, by the restrictions of lockdown on personal movement.

  - → New types of synthetic drugs can emerge that would not necessitate cross-border precursors. Shortages of precursors might not last as soon as international travel is restored.

Cannabis
- ✶ The UN also indicates that lockdown has increased **demand for cannabis**, and that cannabis resin trafficking to Europe is not being disrupted by the restrictions related to the pandemic.

  - → This could intensify drug trafficking activities, including maritime ones, from North Africa to Europe in the future.
  - → Cannabis is often produced locally, near consumer markets, which also implies trafficking will remain unaffected.

Corruption & Infiltration

It is way too early to predict the impact of Covid-19 on the economy and the extent of the economic crisis that could follow the pandemic is still guesswork. The links between this pandemic, its projected effects on the economy and corruption have been already explored[160]. Any attempt to forecast what this could mean for **corruption on the waterfront** is indeed dependent on further data on the following aspect:

* Whether or not **key industries** involved also in the port economy will suffer from the pandemic aftermath. For example, whether or not truck companies struggling during lockdown will be able to go back to work and whether or not there will be the need for **cash** influxes to save some of these companies.
    → This might have an influence in what type of businesses can be exploited for logistics, transport and deliveries in and out of the port.
    → This might also facilitate the possibility of criminal groups, able to invest cash, to buy these companies out of bankruptcies, which eventually will give those groups an advantage in the industry.
* If changes in the workforce of the port, and difficulties in organising rotas, and maintain services in a crisis where rules of social distancing and sickness leaves become the

---

[160] https://www.oecd.org/corruption/the-global-response-to-the-coronavirus-pandemic-must-not-be-undermined-by-bribery.htm ; https://www.u4.no/publications/corruption-in-the-time-of-covid-19-a-double-threat-for-low-income-countries

norm this will have short and medium terms effects on individual corruption:
- → There might be the need to find new 'doors' and/or to change routes if a shortage or a difficulty to find reliable workers or agents at the port becomes a more stable effect of the pandemic in the next months.

✱ In some cases of crisis, some government tend to believe that there is value in scrapping anti-corruption regulations to favour trade and commerce by speeding up procedures.
- → Should this be the case, port authorities need to be extra careful in the allocation of contracts in the port and on the management of senior staff appointments.

Further reading

For research on ports, corruption and organised crime (general)

Blakey, GR and R. Goldstock, On the Waterfront": RICO and Labor Racketeering. *Scholarly Works. Paper 23.* Available for download at: http://scholarship.law.nd.edu/law_faculty_scholarship/23, 1980.

Block, A.A. On the waterfront revisited: The criminology of waterfront organized crime. *Contemporary Crises* 6(4): 373–396, 1982

Jacobs, J.B., and Peters, E., 2003. *Labor racketeering: The mafia and the unions.* Crime and justice, 30, 229–282.

Jacobs, JB., 2006, *Mobsters, unions, and feds: the Mafia and the American labor movement,* New York; London: New York University Press.

Sergi, A. (2020), Policing the Port, Watching the City. Manifestations of Organised Crime in the Port of Genoa, *Policing & Society: An International Journal of Research and Policy,* Online First, https://doi.org/10.1080/10439463.2020.1758103

UNODC. (2013). *Combating transnational organized crime committed at sea.* New York. At https://www.unodc.org/documents/organized-crime/GPTOC/Issue_Paper_-_TOC_at_Sea.pdf

For research on border corruption and security

Andreas P (2003) Redrawing the line: Borders and security in the twenty-first century. *International Security* 28(2): 78–111.

Cowen D (2007) Struggling with 'security': National security and labour in the ports. *Just Labour: A Canadian Journal of Work and Society* 10: 30–44.

Hardy, S.K., *Navigating Through Corruption: An Analysis of Anti-Corruption Criminal Laws in the Port Setting and the BIMCO Anti-Corruption Clause for Charter Parties*, 2017

Jancsics, D., Border Corruption. *Public Integrity* 21(4): 406–419, 2019

For research on port security, port policing and crime

Brewer, R., *Policing the Waterfront. Networks, Partnerships and the Governance of Port Security,* Oxford: Oxford University Press, 2014.

Chalk, P., 2008. *The maritime dimension of international security: terrorism, piracy and the challenges for the United States.* Santa Monica: RAND Corporation.

Christopher, K., 2015. *Port security management.* Boca Raton, FL: CRC Press/Taylor & Francis

Côté-Boucher K (2016) The paradox of discretion: Customs and the changing occupational identity of Canadian border officers. *British Journal of Criminology* 56(1): 49–67.

De Boeck, Arne, Reniers Genserik, Marc Cools, Marleen Easton, and Evelien Van den Herrewegen. 2014. "Optimizing Security Policies and Practices in the Port of Antwerp: Actors' Perceptions and Recommendations." *International Journal of Safety and Security Engineering* 4 (1): 1–16.

Demeri, MJ., The 'watchdog' agency: fighting organized crime on the waterfront of New York and New Jersey. *New England Journal on Criminal and Civil Confinement* 38: 257–279, 2012.

Dinchel, Eva-Katharina, and Marleen Easton, 2020. "Going with the Flow: Comparative Research on Transnational Port Security" In *Policing Transnational Crime: Law Enforcement of Criminal Flows.*, ed by. Saskia Hufnagel and Anton Moiseienko. London: Routledge.

Easton, Marleen, and Fien Gilleir. 2013. "Nodal Aspects of the Surveillance of Transit Migration in Belgian Harbours." *In Crime, Security and Surveillance*: Effects for the Surveillant and the Surveilled, ed. Gudrun Vande Walle , Nils Zurawski , and Evelien Van den Herrewegen The Hague, The Netherlands: Boom-publisher.

Elkwall, D., 2009. The displacement effect in cargo theft. *International journal of physical distribution & Logistics management*, 39 (1), 47–62.

Eski, Y., 'Port of call': Towards a criminology of port security. *Criminology & Criminal Justice* 11(5): 415–431, 2011

Eski, Y., *Policing, Port security and crime control. An ethnography of the port securityscape,* New York: Routledge, 2016.

Eski, Y., Customer is king: promoting port policing, supporting hypercommercialism. *Policing and Society* 30(2): 153–168, 2020.

Eski, Y. and Carpenter, A., Policing in EU seaports: Impact of the ISPS code on port security post-9/11. In: M. O'Neill, K. Swinton and A. Winter (eds.) *New challenges for the EU internal security strategy* Newcastle upon Tyne: Cambridge Scholars Publishing, 71-95, 2013.

Nguyen T (2012) Changes to the role of US Customs and Border Protection and the impact of the 100% container scanning law. *World Customs Journal* 6(2): 109–118.

Madsen, C., (2018) Pacific Gateway: state surveillance and interdiction of criminal activity on Vancouver's Waterfront. *Salus Journal* 6(1): 26-43.

McNicholas, M. (2008) *Maritime security: an introduction.* Amsterdam; Boston: Elsevier/Butterworth Heinemann,

Zhang X and Roe M (2019) Maritime Container Port Security: USA and European Perspectives. New York: Springer.

For research on drug trafficking, ports and maritime routes

Bartilow HA and Eom K (2009) Free traders and drug smugglers: The effects of trade openness on states' ability to combat drug trafficking. *Latin American Politics and Society* 51(2): 117–145.

Calderoni F (2012) The structure of drug trafficking mafias: The 'Ndrangheta and cocaine. *Crime, Law and Social Change* 58(3): 321–349.

Easton, M. 2020. "Policing Flows of Drug in the Harbor of Antwerp: A Nodal-Network Analysis." *In Maritime Supply Chains*, ed by. Thierry Vanelslander. Elsevier.

Eski, Y and R. Bujit, Dockers in drugs: policing the illegal drug trade and port employee corruption in the port of Rotterdam. *Policing: A Journal for Policy and Practice* 11(4): 371-386, 2016.

Hughes CE, Chalmers J and Bright AD (2020) Exploring interrelationships between high-level drug trafficking and other serious and organised crime: An Australian study. *Global Crime*. 21:1, 28-50,

Sergi A. (2020), Playing Pac-Man in Portville: Policing the Fragmentation and Dilution of Drug Importations through Major Seaports, *European Journal of Criminology*, Online First, https://doi.org/10.1177/1477370820913465

Zaitch, D., From Cali to Rotterdam: perceptions of Colombian cocaine traffickers on the Dutch port. *Crime, Law and Social Change* 38(3): 239-266, 2002a.

For research on illicit trade (and maritime routes)

Clarke RV and Brown R (2003) International trafficking in stolen vehicles. *Crime and Justice* 30: 197–227.

Greenberg, M.D., et al., 2006. *Maritime terrorism: risk and liability*. Santa Monica: RAND Corporation.

Liss, C., 2011. *Oceans of crime: maritime piracy and transnational security in Southeast Asia and Bangladesh*. Singapore: ISEAS Publishing.

Nordstrom, C., 2007. *Global outlaws: crime, money, and power in the contemporary world*. Berkeley: University of California Press.

Smith A (2017) Containerization of contraband: Battling drug smuggling at the fourth busiest container handling facility in the United States. *Georgia Journal of International & Comparative Law* 45: 299–313.

For research on the port-city interface

Andrade, M.J., and Costa, J.P., 2020. Touristification of European port-cities: impacts on local populations and cultural heritage. In: A. Carpenter, and R. Lozano, ed. *European port cities in transition. Moving towards more sustainable sea transport hubs.* Amsterdam: Springer International, 67–89.

Bottalico, A., Antwerp and Genoa. Two ports in transition between traditional labour systems and global production networks. *Etnografia e ricerca qualitative*, 2, 2019.

Daamen, T.A., and Louw, E., 2016. The challenge of the Dutch port-city interface. *Journal of economic and social geography*, 107 (5), 642–651.

Daamen, T.A., and Vries, I., 2013. Governing the European port–city interface: institutional impacts on spatial projects between city and port. *Journal of transport geography*, 17, 4–13.

Ducruet, C., 2007. A metageography of port-city relationships. In: J.J. Wang, et al., eds. *Ports, cities, and global supply chains*. Aldershot: Ashgate, 21–35.

Huybrechts, M, 2002, *Port competitiveness: an economic and legal analysis of the factors determining the competitiveness of seaports*. Antwerp: De Boeck.

Mah, A., 2014, *Port cities and global legacies. Urban identity, Waterfront work and radicalism,* London: Palgrave Macmillan.

Van den Berghe, K.B.J., and Daamen, T.A., 2020. From planning the port/city to planning the port-city: exploring the economic interface in European port cities. In: A. Carpenter, and R. Lozano, eds. *European port cities in transition. Moving towards more sustainable sea transport hubs.* Amsterdam: Springer International, 69–84.

Wang, J., et al., 2007. Ports, cities, and global supply chains. Hampshire: Ashgate Publishing Ltd.

Back Cover Matters

Funding
This work was supported by The British Academy [grant number IC3\100276].

ORCID iD
Anna Sergi https://orcid.org/0000-0001-9995-117X

Copyright
The Author
Dr Anna Sergi
University of Essex

About The Author
Anna Sergi, LL.M-, Ph.D.

Anna Sergi holds a PhD in Sociology (2014), with specialisation in Criminology, from the Department of Sociology at the University of Essex. Her research specialism is in organised crime studies and comparative criminal justice. She has published extensively in renowned peer-review journals in criminology on topics related to Italian mafias both in Italy and abroad as well as on policing strategies against organised crime across states. She has authored three monographs on these topics. Since September 2015 she lectures in criminology at the University of Essex.

Photo: Melbourne, DP World, March 2020, Author's rights

Printed in Great Britain
by Amazon

56467204R00131